To
My grandchildren, Shauna and Drew
Whose summer visits to Cape Ann are among my greatest pleasures

Mel,
Enjoy this story.
Merry Xmas.
love
Ceth
'98

ISBN 1-889193-04-6

Cover design and illustrations by Michael Stoffa

Printed by The Pressroom Printers, Gloucester, Massachusetts 01930

Table of Contents

Acknowledgments

Mason Walton had many friends during his long life experience. In death it appears he has many as well. Some are native Cape Anners whose parents and grandparents knew the hermit personally; others met him through his writings and "by reputation." I'd like to thank those who encouraged me to tell the story of this humble man's extraordinary life and others who made it possible.

I begin with the historians in Maine who helped trace Walton's roots from the green hills of Ireland to a village in Nova Scotia to the bustling mill town of Old Town, beside the winding Penobscot River—Elizabeth Buck of Old Town, the late Genevieve Violette of Milford and Amos Kimball of Hampden-Newburg. A special note of gratitude is due Elford H. Messer at the Maine Historical Society in Portland.

On Cape Ann I received friendly, competent assistance from Ellen Nelson at the Cape Ann Historical Association, John W. Crowningshield and Mariam Carter at the Magnolia Historical Society, Reginald Foster at the Manchester Historical Society, Steve Rask and his staff at the Rockport Public Library, Judy Oski at the Gloucester Lyceum and Sawyer Free Library, and Priscilla D. Runkle of the historic Sargent-Murray-Gilman-Hough House Association. Historian Joe Garland and field biologist Ted Tarr also made valuable contributions.

Through the efforts of archivists at the Boston Public Library, I was able to read Walton's original columns which appeared in *Forest and Stream,* and with help from Philip Bergen, Librarian at the Boston Society, I walked in the hermit's shadow as he toured that historic city at the close of the 19th century.

I would also like to thank fellow nature-lover Chuck Reynolds who joined me on explorations of Ravenswood, Greg Chanis, the park's superintendent, and naturalist Bob Speare of the Massachusetts Audubon Society, whose knowledge of natural history was of immense help in reviewing Walton's writings. Lastly, my deep appreciation goes to Dorothy Ramsey Stoffa who read the manuscript, corrected when necessary and inspired continually, and to Michael Stoffa for his creative contributions.

Introduction

Exploring Ravenswood Park in Gloucester, Massachusetts with my Sunday walking group on a cool July morning several years ago, I saw a bronze tablet fronting a large boulder where a footpath intersected with a wide gravel roadway. On it were the words:

In the cabin near this spot
Mason Walton
"Hermit of Gloucester"
Lover of Nature
Lived for
Thirty-Three Years
This Tablet Placed by
Gloucester Woman's Club
1933

The cabin had long since been destroyed by fire but my interest in Walton was piqued at that moment. Who was the man behind the cold, hard facts noted on the plaque, this lover of nature, who lived alone for thirty-three years in the wilderness? I wondered. At the time I was writing another book, *Walking Cape Ann*, and the region's flora and fauna were an important part of my research. Almost mystically, the man on the stone became a kindred spirit.

Who was he? I asked myself as I returned alone to his cabin site again and again. What were the circumstances that brought him to this beautiful primeval forest, and why did he remain for thirty-three years to live out his life alone among the creatures of the wild?

In researching his background, I learned about his family and friends, what his boyhood was like, the name of his favorite teacher and the type of student he was. I followed his interests and activities as he matured into manhood. I explored his avenues of philosophical thought and the circumstances that shaped his life, a life that experienced both the valleys of despair and the heights of national fame.

In life Walton had many friends, among them Cyrus Hamlin, son of Hannibal Hamlin, Vice President of the United States during Abraham Lincoln's first term; General Benjamin Butler, controversial Civil War hero, Congressman, Governor and presidential candidate; the family of Louis Sockalexis, a Penobscot Indian for whom the Cleveland Indians Baseball Team is named; Frank Bolles, nature writer and Secretary of Harvard University, and young John Hays Hammond, Jr., one of

America's greatest inventors, of whom Walton once said, "He's a very clever young lad."

The persona of Mason Walton, the man, could not possibly be projected onto the simple memorial stone in Ravenswood Park. He was a person of great intellect and gentle sensitivity. He contributed much to the academic study of natural history from his little hut deep in the Ravenswood forest. Through his simple stories of life among the animals which he called his "wild friends," he awakened many to the nuances of nature.

His is a fascinating life story. This obscure hermit, who in its purest sense was not a hermit at all, emerged onto the national scene as a highly-respected man of science. Through his nature essays, which appeared in newspapers, magazines and a book, his treasury of information on New England flora and fauna—especially the intelligence of wild animals—became well known. Listed in the first volume of *Who's Who in America,* he was consulted by many in the field of natural science from some of the finest colleges, universities, museums and laboratories throughout the then forty-eight states.

But not everyone agreed with Walton's views on natural history, including naturalist John Burroughs and big-game hunter President Theodore Roosevelt. At issue were actions and behavior Walton attributed to animal intelligence, Burroughs felt to be merely animal instinct, a conflict which even today has not been settled by scientists in this field. Although Roosevelt challenged a number of Walton's stories about the behavior of certain individual birds and animals, he agreed with the hermit and others concerning the reasoning powers of wildlife. This was contrary to Burroughs' position which negated intelligence, psychology and sentiment in the lower species. Labeled by Burroughs as a "romantic naturalist," Walton was in good company, his co-defendants being nature writers Jack London, William Long, Ernest Seton and Charles Roberts. The controversy, which became a heated literary debate lasting five years, was fought in the pages of many important national publications, including the *New York Times*, *The Atlantic Monthly* and *Time* magazine.

All the episodes in this book are based on fact and historical record and every name is the real name of a person who touched Mason Walton's life—many playing a major role—from the time of his birth in Old Town, Maine on July 31, 1838 until his death in Gloucester, Massachusetts on May 21, 1917.

Helen Naismith
Rockport, Massachusetts
Fall 1997

"Me seeum many lobbins in these woods."

Chapter 1
Early Life in Maine

Like many early Americans, Samuel and Sarah Walton were eager to provide a good life for themselves and their children. In the early 1800s, they packed their modest belongings and left Ireland to begin life anew in New Brunswick, Canada. From there, they made their way down to Old Town, Maine, where life began for their little boy Mason on the last day of July 1838. In contrast to his three boisterous brothers Alfred, George and Brainard, and two lively sisters Isabella and Angela, Mason was a quiet, sensitive child.

Old Town was a seven-mile stretch along the Penobscot River north of Bangor. This historic community goes back hundreds of years into the prehistoric days of the Red Paint People, whose ancient settlements preceded those of the Penobscot Indians. The Penobscots are a tribe of North American Indians whose homeland lies along the Penobscot River and Penobscot Bay. While speaking the Algonquian language, they are most closely affiliated with the Passamaquoddy, fellow members in the Abnaki confederacy. An agricultural and fishing people, the Penobscots were traditionally organized into about 14 villages, each consisting of a few hundred people.

The population of Old Town when the Waltons arrived was composed largely of native-born Americans, with only a sprinkling of Canadian, French and Irish immigrants. Progress soon turned the locale into a bustling mill town, as powerful lumber operators harvested thousands of acres of timber from surrounding forests. The newcomers came to fell and trim trees and transport logs from forest lands to sawmills (pine for lumber, poplar for paper). Maine's numerous waters provided ready transportation and the falls at Old Town powered the sawmills that sprang up along the Penobscot River before the advent of steam power. When the booms above Old Town were full, they contained more than six hundred acres of logs. Just before the Civil War, Old Town was producing more lumber than any other town in the United States.

The infant Mason grew into a small-framed boy with light, sandy-colored hair and twinkling blue-gray eyes. Although his head gave the impression of being large, his facial features were small. His nose was thin and just the least bit sunken. The cheek bones, noticeable, but not prominent, seemed to be the dividing line between the small, clean-cut lower jaw and the big forehead and head. Perhaps, to make up for his less-than-handsome looks, he was blessed with a curious mind and a warm, friendly personality.

Mason loved living on the Penobscot River, just as he learned to love the mysterious wilderness of the Maine woods. Despite a leg injury which left him with a slight limp, his boyhood activities were those of other youngsters in his neighborhood: swimming, canoeing, fishing, hiking, hunting and camping. Most of his growing years were spent with his brothers, but he also played with Indian boys from the island. One in particular was a close friend, a bright-eyed young brave named Socko Sockalexis.

Among Mason's happiest times was a trapping expedition he enjoyed with his father at age seven. A guide named Joe Polis, the son of the Indian Governor, was hired to take them deep into the Maine wilderness. The Polis name meant "Little Paul Bear." A charcoal drawing of a young bear paddling a canoe was the totem which identified the Indian's campsites along the Penobscot River.

On the morning of the hunt, Mason and his father were ferried in a bateau, a small, flat-bottomed boat, to the island reservation where Polis lived. It was the summer of 1845. There was no bark wigwam and no pole displaying the territorial bear totem. Instead, the Polis home was a comfortable two-story, white frame bungalow with black shutters, surrounded by a vegetable garden and fruit trees. The property was neat and well-kept, which made the young boy understand later why this Indian was considered special and even "aristocratic" by townspeople.

The term was well-suited to the demeanor of Joe Polis. Dignified and reserved, he presented an imposing, almost regal, figure. He had a broad face and perfect Indian features and complexion. His stout frame was of medium height and exhibited strength and agility. His clothes were those of an ordinary lumberman—red flannel shirt, woolen pants and a black Kossuth hat.

The legendary son of Little Paul Bear usually withdrew into a strange remoteness around the white men he led on hunting expeditions. But early in the Walton hunt, he sensed a kindred spirit in the small boy trailing behind him and opened his eyes and ears to many sights and sounds in the Maine woods. He taught young Mason that animals and birds, like humans, were intelligent and communicated with each other. In clipped, broken English, many of his words ending in the characteristic "um," Polis patiently explained the different vocalizations of birds. These sounds, Indians believed, were messages to other birds—announcing a food source, claiming territory and warning of predators.

At first Mason had difficulty understanding Polis because his "r's" sounded like "l's." But the youngster listened closely and soon realized the Indian meant "robin" when he said, "Me seeum many lobbins in these woods."

The woodthrush, which Polis called by its Indian name, *Adelungquamooktum*, was quite common in Maine forests, he told his young charge. As he listened, Mason tuned his ear to hear its *ee-oh-lay* flute-like song. Later Polis drew his attention to the drumming of a ruff grouse, which to the boy's untrained ear seemed an unusual sound for a songbird. Polis had Indian names for all the birds they saw on the hunt, and could imitate many—from the non-musical rattle of the belted kingfisher's flight call to the cheerful, lengthy carol of the red-breasted "lobbin."

Twelve years later, Thoreau called upon this highly-respected guide to lead him and his friend Edward Hoar into these same woods, the deepest wilderness the Concord naturalist would ever explore. Polis remained one of Thoreau's major heroes.

The paths of Thoreau and Walton would cross again—separated by time—in a magnolia swamp in West Gloucester, Massachusetts. Thoreau's visit took place on a beautiful fall day in September 1858. Walton's came later and lasted longer; it became his home for thirty-three years.

Beginning with his early years at Old Town's Old Grammar School, Mason showed promise of scholastic excellence. His teacher was Miss Helen Hunt, an old-fashioned school marm. In challenging him to study and learn about the world around him, she could not have found a more willing pupil. He had an aptitude for learning and disciplined himself at a very early age to form good study habits.

Understandably, growing up in the culture of his time and place, young Mason's focus was on life in the Maine wilderness. He remembered Joe Polis telling him about birds and animals being able to communicate with each other, and began to observe the wildlife he saw on hunts with his father. He had many opportunities as the forests were inhabited by partridge, deer, moose, caribou, beaver, otter, black cat, sable and Canada lynx; and many rabbits, squirrels and skunks ran around Old Town.

During hikes with friends, he stood silent to catch the high, raspy *queer, queer* sound of the red-headed woodpecker or the raucous *caw, caw, caw* of crows, because now he knew their birdcalls had meaning. In the early spring, after a long, harsh Maine winter, he noticed the migration of birds and animals coming out of hibernation. As warm days and nights approached, he listened for the duck-like call of wood frogs and the "popping" calls of chipmunks—sounds that sparked and held his attention. He also took an interest in wildflowers and plants which grew in woodlands and along the river—the black snake-root, great purple orchis, meadowsweet, wild yellow lily and Canada thistle.

When Mason was still young, his family moved to neighboring Alton, a sleepy, sparsely-settled farming community. It was quite different from Old Town with its friendly Indians, busy sawmills and the ever-flowing Penobscot River. But the Walton children adapted quickly to the change and easily made new friends, including pretty Olive Bradford who lived nearby.

They continued to attend school in Old Town where Miss Hunt took a special interest in Mason. When he was fifteen, she encouraged his parents to send him to Hampden Academy, a private, four-year prep school south of Bangor. As organized school systems developed, these regional academies were established throughout New England to prepare promising students for college. Because of their excellent scholastic programs, they served well the needs of many who didn't have the time or money for higher education. Today Hampden Academy, founded in 1803, is listed on the National Register of Historic Places, thus preserving the heritage of these early educational institutions.

At the academy, Mason's intellect was broadened by a classical study course— Greek, Latin, philosophy, literature, math, science, geology, as well as algebra and geometry. In addition to English literature, the works of American writers emerging onto the literary scene became part of his curriculum. But it was Henry David Thoreau to whom he looked later for books on natural history. He found he had much in common with the man from Walden Pond as he studied botany and ornithology. Many years later Mason would be described as a "Thoreau-type naturalist" and "Mark Twain look-alike," which must have pleased him as he had much in common with both men.

Self-discipline and study proved to be Mason's strong points at Hampden. Even though a high achiever, he took time to be friendly and was well-liked by fellow students. One in particular influenced his life, both during and after their school years. His name was Cyrus Hamlin. During registration Mason and Cyrus were assigned to be seat-mates, sharing a common desk and bench. As such they were teamed together for most school activities and became good friends.

Both boys were serious about their educations and were very studious. In their free time, Cyrus invited Mason to the Hamlin farm a short distance from the academy. But these times were not all fun and games. Cyrus's politically-active father liked farm work, spending many hours in the fields when he was in Hampden—a practice he passed on to his four sons which they, too, enjoyed. When Cyrus and Mason finished their chores, they often walked along the Penobscot River at the edge of the Hamlin property, discussing critical issues in which the family statesman was involved.

At the time Hannibal Hamlin was enjoying a successful political career, having served in both the U.S. House of Representatives and the U.S. Senate, and having represented both political parties. While the boys were at Hampden Senator Hamlin renounced his Democratic allegiance and went over to the Republicans. Shortly before their graduation in 1859, he began a new term in the Senate under his new party affiliation.

Hamlin's increasing prominence and anti-slavery position, together with the political needs of 1860, made him a logical running mate for Abraham Lincoln. He served with distinction during the Emancipator's historic first term. But the course of American history was altered dramatically when Andrew Johnson, an uneducated "war Democrat" from Tennessee, replaced him on the ticket in 1864. This came about when delegates to the Republican Convention felt the need for support from Democrats who had joined Lincoln's position on slavery. It was an ironic twist of fate for the politically astute Hamlin who had been a Democrat all his life. Now, as a Republican supporting the policies of his Republican president, he was ousted by a Democrat in order for his party to gain further support from the opposition for those same guiding principles.

The Civil War caused suffering to families on both sides of that tragic conflict. His leg injury prevented Mason from joining the militia along with his three brothers. But he kept up with the battles in which they fought while he was farming and teaching at a common school. The news from Virginia regarding the Peninsula Campaign of 1862 was not good. George, a cavalry man with Maine's Eleventh Regiment, was killed at the Battle of Fair Oaks. A short time later Brainard was lost at sea while serving with the Navy. Only Alfred, an infantryman, returned home safely.

The sadness of the war visited Mason again two years after the truce was called. His friend Cyrus Hamlin had volunteered to command Negro troops against the Rebels. His officers and men fought valiantly in combat, resulting in Hamlin's advancement to major-general. After the war, he remained in New Orleans commanding the state militia. The Republican party of Louisiana intended to nominate him for governor in 1867. But when the convention assembled, the news came that General Hamlin, a bachelor, had been taken ill with yellow fever. He died after a brief illness at age thirty-one.

Following graduation from the academy, Mason took time to decide what to do with his life. Because he liked the outdoors, his first summer was spent aboard a fishing schooner in the waters off the coast of Maine. But when it was over, he knew he didn't want to be a fisherman; he liked the land more than the sea. He became a teacher and bought a fifteen-acre farm near Pickerel Pond in Penobscot County and began to raise chickens and fresh vegetables. As a hobby he took up bee lining, which he considered more exciting than golf.

Although farming and teaching kept him busy, Mason sought further expression of his energy and intellect. He found it in the Greenback Party, a political movement started in 1868. Desiring expansion of paper money, or "greenbacks," issued by the federal government to finance the Civil War, the independent movement hoped to benefit farmers and the working class. Its leaders opposed the political philosophies of the Whigs, Republicans and Democrats which they felt favored the wealthy, since only they were empowered with gold and silver coins.

Mason became an enthusiastic campaign organizer for the neophyte reformers in 1870, speaking at public rallies and editing the party's campaign newsletter, *The Greenbacker*. Articulate and well-informed on the goals of the movement, he made a lasting impression on voters as he stumped for candidates along the eastern coast of Maine, New Hampshire and Massachusetts. Like his mentor, Hannibal Hamlin, he hated slavery and spoke out against it at every opportunity. He supported the working class, closely following local and regional economic trends that affected people in his area.

It was about this time that philosophical theories advanced at the academy nudged his thoughts in another direction, awakening him to an 18th century movement called *The Freethinkers*. Followers of this sect rejected a supernatural authority and, instead, applied rules of reason and logic to man's moral and religious views. It was a concept he would continue to embrace throughout most of his life.

During this time Mason made frequent visits to his family in Alton. On one of these trips, he noticed that his sisters' friend Olive Bradford had matured into an attractive young lady. Like Mason, she was intellectually inquisitive. Their friendship blossomed into romance and they were married in 1870. Mason was thirty-two when he and his new bride began life together on his Penobscot County farm.

It was a happy marriage. Olive brought a woman's touch to the farmhouse and companionship to her husband. Like Mason, she loved the outdoors and they often hiked together in the Maine woods. In the evenings after supper they relaxed on the porch and watched the moon cresting over the distant mountains.

Unfortunately, their wedded bliss was short-lived. In the seventh year of life together, Olive died in childbirth. The baby, a girl, lived only a few hours. Mason was grief-stricken as he walked behind the horse-drawn caskets to the family burial plot in Alton where they were laid to rest.

In time the lonely widower picked up the threads of his life. He became editor of *The Bangor Record*, but soon left this position to join a Bangor pharmaceutical firm as an accountant. And he returned to work behind the scenes in politics, again in support of the Greenback Party.

When the drug company moved its headquarters to Boston in 1880, Mason was asked to head its delinquent accounts section. Despite the changes he knew he'd have to make, he accepted and reluctantly put his farm up for sale. As he packed his meager belongings, he could not have realized how much his future life in Massachusetts would be influenced by his boyhood experiences in the woods of Maine.

Chapter 2
Nature Heals when Medicine Fails

A warm spring day greeted Walton's arrival in Boston. After a few inquiries, he found a small room a short distance from his company's new offices at the Customs House. During his free time, he explored his new surroundings and the far reaches of the city to view Boston's historic landmarks. His tours took him from the narrow, cramped streets of the North End to the wide avenues curving down to Beacon Street.

Loving nature as he did, Walton was drawn to the city's popular twin parks, Boston Common and the Public Garden.

The promenade along the Common was created in colonial times for the "domestic amusement" of proper Bostonians who enjoyed a pleasant walk after their afternoon tea. In the winter the site became a beautiful winter wonderland, and on days off, Walton often braved the ice and snow to watch youngsters toboggan down its long, sloping paths.

In the warm weather he spent many sunny afternoons in the Public Garden which was more formal than the Common. Lining the south side of Beacon Street, it was a refreshing oasis between residential Back Bay and the downtown business district. The Garden contained beautiful plants, shrubs, flowers, a large conservatory and a calm, reflective pond winding snake-like through the grounds carrying happy children in graceful swan boats.

Walton busied himself at the pharmaceutical company. His life in Boston was different from what he'd known in rural Maine. He loved the rugged wilderness for which his native state was known, but he also appreciated the history, culture and architectural beauty of the bayside metropolis. Each day he passed through the rotunda of the Customs House, awed by its splendor. From his desk on the first floor, he could glance out the window upon the harbor where packet boats, an early version of the commuter ship, tied up just outside the front door. At lunch time, he often walked along the wharves and listened to the daily auctions of the fishing fleet's catch. In time, he began to adjust to his new circumstances.

The political patronage of Massachusetts state government was well known, and Boston was the hub of the wheel that rolled the political machinery throughout the Commonwealth. When Walton arrived on the scene, reform was taking place in the Bay State as it had been back home in the Pine Tree State. In 1881 both the Democratic and the National Greenback-Labor State Conventions nominated sixty-four-year-old Benjamin F. Butler, a controversial Civil War general and former

Lowell congressman, to be their gubernatorial candidate. Since he had embraced the Greenback movement in Maine, it was natural for Walton to support Butler's race for governor. Although his leanings were Republican and Independent, for him, it was a matter of principle that guided his political philosophy. Just as he had supported Lincoln, a Republican, in freeing slaves, he now supported Butler, a Democrat, who pledged to improve conditions for the underprivileged. He was well-informed about critical issues facing the country, a fact duly noted by Butler supporters who began to respect the intelligent, politically-savvy idealist from the backwoods of Maine.

Between chasing bad debts by day and speaking at rallies late into the night, Walton kept busy. He had become an avid proponent of social reform which he felt could be achieved only through political activism. His long hours on the campaign trail were rewarded on November 8, 1882 when "brave Old Ben Butler" was elected Governor of Massachusetts.

Not long after the election, Walton experienced a series of health problems, which began with a respiratory infection. Except for his leg injury, he'd had relatively good health all his life, and at first didn't attach too much importance to a lingering cough. He worked daily at the drug firm despite a feeling of weariness. Then he began to lose weight and was constantly wheezing and coughing.

The diagnosis was "catarrh, malignant, persistent," an inflammation of a mucus membrane resulting in chronic allergies and coughing, combined with "dyspepsia, aggravated." The condition caused him to have a dull, heavy pain of indigestion when he ate. He had to spray his nose and throat every morning to relieve severe facial pain. His lungs were sore and the palms of his hands hot and dry. Soon he lost so much weight that his body wasted away to a mere skeletal form. He was advised by a physician to leave the city and go into the woods to try life in a pine grove. But, because he had no money to pay for this medical advice, Walton discarded it as kind, but meaningless.

He remembered the summer he'd spent on the fishing schooner in the waters off the Maine coast. During that time he'd been completely free of seasickness and, in fact, even gained weight. As he lay sick and discouraged in his rooming house, his thoughts returned again and again to the sea voyage. To him that schooner had been a natural sanitarium, improving his health as it had. He believed a few weeks on salt water would, in fact, do wonders for his health now.

With renewed hope, the sick man packed his bag on a hot, humid August morning in 1884 and made his way to the Boston pier. Paying the fifty-cent fare, he slowly climbed the plank and boarded the *City of Gloucester* steamer for the 10 o'clock sailing. Weak and listless, he clung to the railing of the black, stubby, high-sided craft as it plowed the waters northward to Cape Ann.

Two hours later, he arrived at Steamboat Wharf at the foot of Duncan Street in Gloucester where the previous day a fire at the Harvey & Tarr Manufacturing Company destroyed seventeen buildings along the harbor. The devastation and charred ruins added to Walton's depression. That afternoon he tried to gain passage aboard one of the mackerel boats making short trips out of the harbor. In offering to pay his own way, he felt he'd find a skipper willing to take him. But he was wrong.

"We're going after fish," he was told more than once, "and cannot be bothered with a sick man."

For three days he haunted the wharves, but to no avail. Finally, he approached a bearded, leather-skinned sea captain who told him brusquely, "I once took a sick man on board. Because we did not strike fish, the fishermen called him a Jonah, and made his life miserable. Three days after we returned, he died and I swore then I'd never take another sick man to sea."

The officer's story ended Walton's search for his "natural sanitarium" on the high seas. Disappointed and dejected, he abandoned the salt water cure and turned instead to the hills around Gloucester, selecting a grassy plot on Bond Hill. The spot was located in a 300-acre primeval forest of hemlock, pine and cedar. Here he pitched a small, cotton tent bought from a shopkeeper on Main Street. He hoped the salt of the ocean and the balsam of the forest would restore his health. Like Emerson who left Harvard Divinity School to seek relief from poor health and failing eyesight at his uncle's Newton farm, Walton hoped to find similar comfort in the coastal woods of Gloucester.

Cape Ann juts out to sea along the eastern coast of Massachusetts about thirty-five miles north of Boston. Waters of Massachusetts Bay wash its southern shore and Ipswich Bay its northern; the towns of Essex and Manchester form its western boundary. Its surface is uneven, with ledges, rocky hills and granite "erratics" left from the glacier that passed the region about 12,000 years ago.

Gloucester was incorporated as a "fishing plantation" in 1639, taking its name from an English town from which many of the settlers came. When Walton arrived on Cape Ann on that steamy August afternoon in 1884, Gloucester was enjoying the reputation of being the leading center for the cod, mackerel and halibut fisheries and ranked first in the world in fishing.

In the woods around Bond Hill, Walton found an ample supply of ripe wild fruit—apples, blueberries and huckleberries. He also found masses of granite towering above a small settlement of cottages at the base of the cliff. He recalled reading about great flocks of eagles nesting in a similar place called "Eyrie," and decided to take the name for his own small domain on Bond Hill.

Apple Row was the name of the long, winding lane leading from Bond Hill down to Western Avenue, a main road into the city of Gloucester. At first Walton managed to walk down this lane to the tea house at the bottom of the hill for his noon meal, bringing back enough food to last until the following day. But climbing back up was very difficult for him. It drained his energy and he had to make three rest stops before reaching his campsite.

During his recuperation, he passed many hours at Eyrie, enjoying the magnificent panoramic view spread before him. He could see a large part of Gloucester, extending in a semicircle from Riverdale to Eastern Point. Later in the season he would watch the ebb and flow of the tide on the marshes bordering the Annisquam River. Also in plain view was the outer harbor, with Ten Pound Island near the entrance of the inner harbor. The shifting scenes on their restless waters held his attention most of the day. At dusk on a warm, still evening in early September, he looked down on more than 500 vessels riding calmly at anchor in the Gloucester Harbor, their lights sparkling brightly from their positions on board.

Day after day he watched the fishing vessels round Eastern Point bound for the open sea. When one returned with her flag at half-mast, he was reminded of the hardships and perils of fishermen whose mortality rate was second only to miners. As he viewed life in the harbor below, he became familiar with the routine of some of the local fishermen. Every morning at daybreak, for instance, he noticed men coming in out of the night, having pulled their lobster pots in the wee hours of the morning. He noticed another lone fisherman sail out of the harbor early each day to fish for shore codfish to support his large family. And fully-laden draggers heading for home escorted by a hovering flock of seagulls also became a familiar sight.

On his left as he faced the harbor, he could look across the marsh to Dogtown Common in the heart of Cape Ann. During Revolutionary days, this was a small pioneer village of seventy-five houses, but in Walton's time, there were no dwellings. The 3,000-acre community had declined to boulder-covered pasture land, blueberry bushes and large tangles of catbrier.

Sunsets from Eyrie were beautiful. As the sun sank behind billowing clouds flushed with pink, windows in the villages glowed like burnished gold. Later, perched on the brow of the cliff, Walton studied the city by moonlight and saw imaginary figures in the shapes of the buildings below. The light at Eastern Point became the blinking red eye of the famed Gloucester sea serpent spotted by many along its shores in the early 1800s. On his right the distant flashes of Thatcher Island's twin lights added drama and mystery to the ever-changing scenery he enjoyed from high atop his eagle's nest. After a rainfall, he enjoyed gazing down onto the misty tops of oaks, maples and hemlocks in the valleys below.

While resting and observing activities beneath Bond Hill, Walton found the berries and apples in the woods around his tent seemed to nourish him. After two weeks of outdoor life, he noticed color returning to his cheeks and his health seemed to be on the mend. One morning he awoke and realized he had not coughed at all during the night. The persistent cough that had made his life so miserable for the past two years in the city was gone. By the end of September, his catarrh had also disappeared, and with it the hay fever symptoms and facial discomfort.

What neither Walton nor his physician realized at the time was that the primary cure for chronic forms of cold, such as asthma, catarrh and bronchitis, is a diet of non-mucus forming foods. The raw, fresh fruits and berries he found in the woods contained no mucoids whatsoever, raw green vegetables very little.

In this spot he called Eyrie, which reminded him of the grace of spreading eagle wings, Walton found his "natural sanitarium," a place where nature healed when medicine failed.

Chapter 3
The General's Last Stand

Meanwhile, as Walton was nursing himself back to health on Bond Hill, Benjamin Butler was spending the summer at his home high above Hodgkins Cove in nearby Bay View contemplating a race for the presidency. It was General Butler who gave this little bayside village its name while camping on its shore with his two sons shortly after the Civil War. He felt the sunsets over Ipswich Bay were as beautiful as those over the Bay of Naples or anywhere else in his travels.

In the summer of 1884 Butler was in the unusual position of having received presidential nominations from both the Anti-Monopoly and Greenback parties. The newly-formed National Party also wanted him as its nominee. Although his stature was enhanced by the attention he received from these minor parties, what he really wanted was the Democratic nomination. But when his liberal platform was voted down at their national convention in Chicago, his support began to fade. Even his own delegates went over to Grover Cleveland. Disappointed but ever the warrior, he accepted the nomination of the Anti-Monopoly and Greenback coalition, which he immediately combined with other minor factions to form the People's Party.

Walton had been following these events with great interest and when "brave Old Ben" announced his candidacy for president on August 29 in Harrisburg, Pennsylvania, his health was well enough for him to join the Butler campaign in mid-September. Because he understood the candidate's political position on key issues, as well as on the platform of the Greenback Party, he became a popular speaker at rallies along coastal Massachusetts. From his campsite on Bond Hill, he traveled the campaign trail from Cape Ann to Cape Cod.

However, on the national scene, the campaign did not go well. Butler preferred doing things his own way and didn't take kindly to too much assistance, nor was he always precise in instructing his campaign managers. The lack of coordination within the supporting parties, coupled with inadequate funding at all levels, hindered the work of his volunteers.

Not surprisingly, Butler was defeated in the 1884 presidential election. He was deeply disappointed in his low vote and felt labor and other people for whom he worked so hard while in office had let him down.

In his declining years, he continued to visit Bay View each summer where he worked on his autobiography, *Butler's Book*.

On January 4, 1893, the old warrior died at his home in the nation's capitol of pneumonia and heart attack. An honor guard escorted the body to Lowell where seventy-five policemen and firemen directed the crowds who came from all over New England to pay their respect. Walton was among them. The General's body was carried in a hearse, drawn by six black-plumed horses, to its final resting place in the family cemetery plot in Dracut.

Chapter 4
As Snug as a Bug in a Rug

Walton lived in the tent he called home from August to December. Camping experiences in the Maine woods helped him adjust to the austerity of his new life. Beans became his staple food, which he baked in a bean-pot over hot coals in a hole in the ground. Bark from dead hemlock trees gave the best coals in the shortest time, he found. After the beans were cooked, the coals remained hot enough to make his coffee. At times the temperature dropped to zero in the cotton tent, and he kept warm by filling two metal milk cans with hot coals from the campfire. By keeping the tent flaps closed, the temperature inside the tent was reasonably comfortable, thanks to his innovative milk-can heaters.

During Walton's first few months at Eyrie, the weather in Gloucester was comparatively mild and the sea calm. But in mid-November a blustery nor'easter appeared on the horizon. When it reached Cape Ann, it unleashed its pent-up fury onto the rocky shore with gale-force winds and heavy rains. The force of the storm was so great that Walton felt the solid rock tremble beneath his tent from the shock of thunderous waves against the headland, a quarter of a mile away.

The powerful storm wrecked his tent. With winter coming, he decided he needed better shelter and looked for a spot protected from the ocean winds. His new campsite was ideal. Located along Old Salem Road on the lower back slope of Bond Hill, it was surrounded by wooded hills, and fresh water from nearby Fuller Brook was another advantage.

Old Salem Road was an old common road originating in Salem and running north-easterly along the south shore of the Cape, through Beverly, Pride's Crossing, Beverly Farms, Manchester, Magnolia, Gloucester's West Parish and harbor, to Rockport. It had been deserted more than a hundred years during Walton's time when it was used only as a wood road in winter. It was also known as the Old Pest House Road because of the small isolation hospital built along its upper Magnolia route to isolate people with smallpox during the mid-1700s. During this time several Negro families lived along the road. On his walks, Mason explored the ruins of seven cellars marking the spots where the dwellings once stood.

Walter Cressey, a prominent townsman, owned forty acres of Gloucester woodland, including Walton's new campsite. One morning following the destructive nor'easter, Walton went into town to find the landowner to gain permission to build a cabin on his property. He found Mr. Cressey very agreeable, even suggesting the removal of a portion of the stone wall straddling Old Salem Road so he (Walton) wouldn't feel hemmed in.

When the cabin was finished, Walton shopped the downtown stores for second-hand furniture. With the help of men from the wharves, he brought back a table, chair, cot, bookcase and stove. During the winter months, the little cabin weathered snow storms and blizzards, but Walton didn't mind. He told his new Gloucester friends he was very comfortable. In his words, he was "as snug as a bug in a rug" in his new cabin home.

December in New England is the month when Mother Nature, like many homeowners, "shuts up house and turns the key." The lower animals, insects and some reptiles, to all appearances, become entirely dormant during the winter and return to life only when food is available to them again. Wild mice, squirrels and chipmunks gather up nuts and grains and take them to hiding places; the wood-chuck and raccoon, having grown fat on the autumn's abundance, roll them-selves up for a long sleep, the woodchuck in his nest, the coon in a den in the rocks. For them and many other creatures of the wild, activity comes to a standstill. They consume little oxygen and live upon the coats of fat they wore into their winter quarters. Deer, like the fox and rabbit, must have food all winter, as evidenced by tell-tale footprints in the snow.

Another way nature preserves wildlife throughout the cold winter months is by migration. As autumn advances, many of the smaller birds that summer on Cape Ann quietly make their way south to find warmer climes and new stores of food. The honks and barks of Canada geese—mated pairs giving alternating calls—come from among the clouds as flocks wend their way south night and day. Long before the journey, they collect their broods in lakes and bays near their breeding grounds and organize for the lengthy trip. For most, it's a first-time flight to a place they have never seen. In every flock leaving their northern habitats, most are young and have flown only a few miles before they embark on that long flight to an unknown land. They follow their guide without hesitation. Which prompts the question, when did the first leader learn the way?

It was during his first winter on Cape Ann that Walton turned his attention to the world of nature, including ornithology, the study of birds. Chickadees, black snowbirds and tree sparrows were frequent visitors to his cabin dooryard and he fed them with different kinds of bird seed. He decided then to devote the rest of his life to the study of his forest environment—its fauna and flora—and share his knowledge with others.

Up on Bond Hill the winter of 1884-1885 gradually melted under many weeks of warm spring sunshine. In April a rejuvenated Walton returned to the shop on Main Street where he bought his tent the previous August. This time he purchased a hammock which he hung between two tall oaks behind the cabin. A tarpaulin placed a few feet above the swing and side panels of cheesecloth protected him from rain and mosquitoes. He slept outside in this canopied bed from April through the first snowfall in November or December.

Exploring the wooded hills in the following weeks, the aspiring naturalist studied vernal ponds, vegetative growth, footprints and feathers with extraordinary perception. Wildflowers began springing up in great profusion in the natural garden that surrounded his cabin and meandered down to Fresh Water Cove. He found the whole area interesting and decided to keep a daily journal of his findings. Just coming into bloom were wood anemones, lady's-slippers, violets, irises, starflowers, the Canada mayflower, clintonia and Indian cucumbers. Bunch berries, partridgeberries (also called twin berries) and wintergreen (teaberries) were scattered amid a ground covering of "gold thread" and star-shaped haircap moss.

The diary also noted he found acres of large skunk cabbage (related to the calla lily), the beautiful rose hardhack or steeple bush, pink meadow-sweet, marsh marigolds, Jack-in-the-pulpit (also related to the white calla), and the Indian pipe, known to many as the corpse plant because of its white, ghost-like color and erect form. There were also several types of holly: inkberry (with black berries), and two deciduous varieties—mountain holly with dull red fruit, and black alder, the common red berry holly. These, along with mosses, ferns, and partridge vine, were carefully examined by Walton and described in his journal.

Among the shrubs and trees growing in the Gloucester woods were sumac, viburnums, mountain laurel, rhododendrons, oak, birch, beech, maple, hemlock and pine. Walton studied the characteristics of each, noting the white, peeling trunk of the paper birch, the texture and number of needles of conifers and the green and white wavy bark of the striped maple. He also noted the shapes of trees, from the egg-shaped red maple to the pyramidal hemlock, and the leaves of hardwoods which likewise varied in shape, as well as in size, texture and color.

Walton discovered a botanical wonder in the sweet-scented, creamy-flowered magnolia growing in the swamp below his cabin. In researching the species, he learned the tall, spindly tree with glossy green leaves was indigenous to Virginia. It was this southern transplant that gave the nearby village (Magnolia) its name. As to how it arrived in the Magnolia swamp, its northern most boundary, Walton suspected either by early settlers or by birds carrying its seed. After flowering, the tree forms bunches of scarlet berry-like fruit hanging from the main stem, attracting birds and the likelihood of propagation. Its common names are sweet swamp, white bay, sweet bay or beaver tree. Evergreen farther south, it's deciduous in Magnolia Swamp, and its large fragrant blossoms peak in early July.

Walton's journal also recorded the myriad birds that visit Cape Ann throughout the year—sparrows, the bay-winged bunting, blackbird, chickadee, yellow-bellied woodpecker, blue-winged yellow warbler, blue jay, wood thrush, hermit thrush, chestnut-sided warbler, pigeon hawk, indigo bird, oven bird, black-throated green warbler, Maryland yellowthroat, red-winged blackbird, brown thrush, Baltimore oriole, belted kingfisher and the great horned owl.

Among the small animals sharing the forest with the feathered tribe were deer-mice, white-footed mice, pine voles, raccoons, woodchucks, chipmunks, flying squirrels, red squirrels, stoats, mink, rabbits, moles and skunks. Walton recorded each time he saw one of these wild creatures scampering across his path, or dashing through the woods at his approach. Some of these entries became sagas as he followed the daily activities of a particular bird or animal whose behavior aroused his curiosity. As he spent more and more time patiently observing their actions, he became attached to some, even giving them pet names. In his journal, for instance, he noted the cleverness of Triplefoot, a three-footed fox he followed all the way across the Cape to Wingaersheek Beach; the loyal companionship of Wabbles, a male song sparrow that woke him at daybreak each morning; and the antics of a fiery red squirrel named Bismarck, which he described as a "disreputable character." Was it instinct or intelligence, he wondered, that governed their patterns of behavior and survival techniques? To satisfy his curiosity, he began a study that lasted the rest of his life.

Gloucester's hermit was soon respected as "a man of superior intelligence, pure character and pleasant disposition."

Chapter 5
The Beginning of Hermit Life

When Gloucester townspeople learned that a stranger had built a cabin on Bond Hill and intended to live there year round, many were curious and made the trip into the woods to meet him. What they found surprised them.

From the beginning, Walton was referred to as "the hermit." But the term was a misnomer. He was not a hermit in the usual sense of the word. Visitors—and there were many—found him friendly and interesting. He was fond of children and patiently answered their questions about the birds and animals seen around his cabin. A few, however, found him frightening, despite his quiet dignity.

When her parents asked the reason for her fear, little six-year old Betty Rogers replied with simple, child-like logic, "because he's an old man and lives all alone in the woods."

However, adults came to respect the cabin-dweller a local reporter described as "a man of superior intelligence, pure character and pleasant disposition."

During his first spring at the hermitage, Walton went to the city daily. After breakfast, which he now cooked on his stove and enjoyed at table, he walked down Bond Hill to attend errands. He soon became a familiar figure along the waterfront where fishermen greeted him warmly when he limped by. Sometimes he stopped to chat at their small fishing shacks as they repaired their nets.

After picking up his mail at the post office and newspapers from a nearby shop, he headed for the public library or the science museum. These were the sources that broadened his intellect, as well as his interest in the activities and culture of the seaside community. He was an avid reader of Cape Ann's newspapers which at the time included the *Gloucester Daily News*, *Cape Ann Advertiser*, *Cape Ann Bulletin* and *Cape Ann Evening Breeze*. These, together with the Sawyer Free Library and the Cape Ann Scientific and Literary Association, linked the friendly "hermit" to the outside world.

A year before Walton's arrival, Samuel Sawyer, a successful Boston businessman, bought the large Georgian style mansion at the corner of Middle Street and Dale Avenue, and had it renovated into a public library. He provided additional funds to furnish the large rooms and stately halls with elegant furnishings, including rare paintings collected during his foreign travels. At the time of its dedication in July 1884, a month before Walton settled on Bond Hill, 6,500 volumes were available to the townspeople. For the erudite newcomer, they became a vital resource in his study of natural history.

Another important learning center for Walton was the Cape Ann Scientific and Literary Association, a block from the library. It occupied the former residence of Captain Elias Davis, whose wife had it built while he was away on a long sea voyage. Like the library, the handsome, square, three-story house provided an ambience of comfort and elegance for the city's culturally-minded.

Walton was drawn to its lectures by naturalists from the Peabody Museum who spoke on many subjects, including American archeology. Of particular interest to him was a talk he attended on the glacial boulders on Dogtown Common.

As a means of furthering his knowledge of natural history, Walton subscribed to a popular weekly journal entitled *Forest and Stream* which aimed "to promote a healthy interest in outdoor recreation and to cultivate a refined taste for objects of nature." [In 1930, it became a magazine and was renamed *Field and Stream*.]

To serve its rural readers, the journal included a mail order section, offering books on a wide range of nature subjects. Walton became a regular customer. The little bookcase in the corner of his cabin soon overflowed with the scholarly works of Charles Darwin, John Muir and English ornithologists, as well as the more subjective writings of Jack London, William Long and Thoreau. The Concord naturalist's stories about tramping the Maine woods and living at Walden Pond held special meaning to Gloucester's hermit because he could relate to both. These books, along with those at the public library and historical association, enriched his life.

In the late 1880s, Walton became a contributor to *Forest and Stream*. Using the nom de plume *The Hermit*, he wrote about his experiences, observations and theories concerning the creatures he encountered in the Cape Ann woods. He considered the birds and animals friends and his simple, folksy stories revealed himself to be a man of extraordinary sensitivity and perception. Theirs was a trusting relationship, enabling Walton to gain insight and knowledge about wildlife which others as yet had not.

Despite this unscientific approach, his writings had great appeal to naturalists, botanists, zoologists, geologists, museum curators, historians and librarians. Letters from all over the country began to arrive in his letter box at the post office, seeking information about the flora and fauna of New England. Some correspondents requested specimens of the unusual sweet bay magnolia growing in Magnolia Swamp. Many, in fact, made personal visits to see for themselves the strange phenomena of the southern magnolia that continued to survive the North's severe winter weather. Others inquired about his research on bird and animal intelligence.

In answering their questions, Walton consulted his daily journals listing details of his botanical and wildlife studies. His cabin contained boxes of dried flora specimens carefully catalogued by groups of wildflowers, weeds, fungi and edible plants. Instances of the reasoning powers of animals were carefully recorded. They had required many hours of silent, persistent observation and note-taking. Each incident included the date, time, place, weather and circumstances under which it occurred. He was precise in this documentation, ever mindful of the importance of accuracy since he knew he was among those blazing new trails in intellectual thought about America's wildlife.

As a result of his dedication and hard work, people of distinction began to regard Gloucester's woodland resident with admiration and respect. To some he was an articulate scholar and philosopher, to others a knowledgeable naturalist—and to a few, including the families of Governor William Russell and wealthy John Hays Hammond, he became a valued friend.

A feature story in the *Boston Globe* one Sunday waxed eloquently about the man on Bond Hill. "High up on an old road, long since discontinued for public travel, in the suburbs of Gloucester, where the fragrance of the magnolia mingles with the incense of the pine, lives one of the best known recluses in New England, if not the country."

In his book *From Blomidon to Smoky*, published in 1894, Harvard Secretary Frank Bolles, an ardent nature lover, also wrote about the Gloucester hermit.

"I have a friend who lives alone, summer and winter, in a tiny hut amid the woods. The doctors told him that he must die, so he escaped from them to nature, made his peace with her, and regained his health. To the wild creatures of the pasture, the oak woods, and the swamps he is no longer a man, but a faun; he is one of their own kind, shy, alert, silent. They, having learned to trust him, have come a little nearer to men."

He also appeared in *Pleasure Drives Around Cape Ann*. "For years he has lived in these dense woods far from all habitation, cultivating the friendship of birds, squirrels, woodchucks, spiders and other natives which claim this spot their home. No more interesting place to visit is there than this of hermit Walton's and no more intelligent person to converse with can be found."

As Walton's reputation grew beyond Cape Ann, people in Gloucester were eager to claim him as their own. High school teachers called upon him to lead field trips for students. Several parents paid him to tutor their youngsters privately. Despite little Betty Rogers' anxiety, he was very popular with the rising generation. In fact, his association with school children resulted in his writing a tender wildlife story for *The Youth Companion*. Early contributors to this national magazine included Harriet Beecher Stowe and Louisa May Alcott. Years later they were joined by two other New Englanders—nature writer Mason Walton and a young illustrator named Norman Rockwell.

Postcards of "The Hermitage, Gloucester, Mass." showing various scenes of Walton and his vine-covered log cabin, began appearing in gift shops and visitor centers along the North Shore. They depicted a man resembling Mark Twain (despite a higher forehead), with curly, white hair and full mustache, of medium height, and slightly bent. He wore a black suit, the jacket unbuttoned exposing a matching vest, and white shirt open at the collar. Around his neck was a colorful kerchief tucked neatly inside the lapels of his jacket. In some photographs, he sat at his desk in the open dooryard, the cabin in the background; in others he was tending his garden with bird houses of every shape and size perched on limbs of nearby trees.

Having learned much about the sciences of natural history through books and field research, the respected Mr. Walton began to lecture throughout New England. His alma mater, the Cape Ann Scientific and Literature Association, asked him to head a section on ornithology. On Saturday, May 5, 1900, he traveled to Boston to address the Hale Natural History Club on Annisquam during the ice age. But it was his work on the intelligence of animal life that gained him a listing in the first volume of *Who's Who in America*, (1887-1942).

Walton's growing stature as a nature writer brought a certain amount of fame, but earnings were another matter. His neat appearance on postcards belied the fact that he lived on the edge of poverty. Resourceful in his efforts to earn living expenses and feed his wildlife friends, he made hockey sticks for local ice skaters, sold flowers (but not vegetables) from his garden and magnolias from the swamp. He also gathered specimens and tagged them with their Latin names for students of botany. And he mounted wildlife when asked, recording in his journal, "one raccoon and many birds and squirrels."

He also worked in fisheries-related businesses along the harbor making seines and twine, anchors, fish glues, boxes and foul weather gear for the fishermen. During this time granite was a thriving industry on Cape Ann, and on occasion he was hired to spread crushed stone along Western Avenue.

In the meantime, a change had taken place in the woods surrounding Magnolia Swamp—a change concerning the spot on Bond Hill where the little cabin stood.

Samuel Sawyer, who had presented the library to the community five years earlier, died in December 1889. When his will was read, it was learned that the philanthropist owned a great deal of property surrounding Fresh Water Cove. He directed that, "None of the numerous woodlots now owned by me, or hereafter purchased are to be sold, or in any way disposed of, but to be retained by my executors and trustees for the protection and beauty of the Cove Village now so called, but sometime in the near future to be laid out handsomely with driveways and pleasant rural walks and then dedicated in the name of 'Ravenswood Park.'"

Characteristically, the generous Mr. Sawyer attached $60,000 to this gift "to be safely invested as heretofore directed and the income only to be used in developing and beautifying the present Ravenswood Park grounds by clearing away the deadwood and other encumbrances, and for the purchasing of other contiguous woodlands, that may be essential in perfecting its present form and completion."

Complying with these instructions, the trustees purchased adjoining woodland, including Mr. Cressey's forty acres along Old Salem Road. The entire area was laid out as a natural park with wide, tree-shaded drives winding through the forest which, after new landlot acquisitions, totaled just under 600 acres. The drives, however, were not intended for carriages, but pedestrian travel only. Footpaths were cut through groves of hemlock, along ridges and down into Magnolia Swamp. A caretaker was employed full-time during eight months of the year and half-time from November through February. Walton was allowed to remain as the only tax-paying resident within the park and henceforth became known as the "Hermit of Ravenswood."

Within a very short time, Ravenswood Park became a popular Cape Ann attraction. Residents and tourists alike were drawn to its sylvan tranquility all seasons of the year. Since Walton's cabin was located on Old Salem Road, the main drive through the park, he, too, grew in popularity. Over the next twenty years visitors to the park—and the hermit's cabin—included famous artists and writers, school teachers and students, and the families of Portuguese fishermen and road builders. Also, foreign ministers from Manchester's summer embassies and wealthy tourists from Cape Ann seaside resorts, as well as distinguished local residents, were among the callers.

The family of John Hays Hammond, a mining engineer extraordinaire, was one of the latter. Over the years Walton watched with admiration and respect as Hammond's son, Jack Jr. emerged from an energetic, imaginative schoolboy into a serious young man of science. He often visited his oceanside laboratory, describing him once as "that clever young lad who invents such wonderful things." Unfortunately, Walton did not live to see the heights to which the youthful Hammond ascended in later years. Hailed as a scientific genius, his achievements, like those of his father, were monumental.

Chapter 6
An Artful Old Coon

Walton's first study of animal intelligence involved "an artful old coon" he called Satan. His notes detailed the characteristics of the raccoon—about the size of a small dog and easily recognized by its black mask and salt-and-pepper coat.

It was under a boulder in Ravenswood that Walton found Satan. He decided to catch him and set a trap covered with leaves at the mouth of his den. In order to prevent injury to the animal's feet, he wound a cloth around the jaws of the trap, to which he attached a clog. The next morning the trap, cloth and clog were gone. Following a zigzag trail through the leaves, he found the frightened raccoon hiding beneath some witch-hazel shrubs, to which he was securely anchored by the clog. Throwing a piece of heavy duck cloth over the animal, trap and all, to protect himself from gnarling teeth and thrusting claws, he toted his squirming captive back to the cabin.

After two hours of struggling desperately, Walton finally managed to put a strap around the raccoon's neck. With the strap securely fastened and attached to a dog-chain, he removed the trap from his prisoner's foot then staked him near the cabin. For two weeks, night and day, the frantic animal tried to free himself, then wearily gave in, resigned to his fate.

"Instinct plays no part in coon lore," Walton wrote of the incident in his journal. "A coon can reason as well as the average human being. My captive proved to be as artful and wicked as Beelzebub himself."

As an example, he noted that when he took his gun into the woods, on his return Satan raced around in his cage eagerly anticipating the squirrel he had not seen, but knew he'd get. When Walton went away without the gun, Satan paid no attention to him on his return.

"Was he guided by scent?" Walton asked himself, and decided to record the direction of the wind on his next few hunts. After several episodes, he believed that scent did not play a role in Satan's actions because on all occasions the wind was blowing in the opposite direction when he returned with his kill.

"Without doubt he connected the gun and squirrel in his mind, and perhaps knew more about a gun than I thought," wrote Walton.

Like all wild animals, Satan did not like being caged. When he worked outside the cabin, Walton chained his captive to a small pine tree. Every morning before leaving for the city, he put him into the cage.

In studying his subject's diet, Walton found that his order of preference was: insects, eggs, birds or poultry, frogs, nuts, red squirrel, rabbit, gray squirrel and fish, which evidently was his bill of fare during his wild state.

One morning, a mink chased an almost-grown rabbit into the dooryard and killed it. When Walton brought it to him for his daily meal, Satan opened the rabbit's mouth with his fore paws and ate out the tongue, after which he skinned the head, turning the skin back over the neck. He then crushed the bones of the head and lapped out the brains. On the third day he finished off the rabbit and the skin was turned inside out, even to the ends of the toes. Squirrels, Walton noted, were skinned in the same manner.

Night after night, during the nutting season, Satan called to other raccoons which answered from surrounding woods. When the sweet acorns were ripe, he was especially active early in the evening as they scurried about in search of food. Scenting them, Satan did his best to attract their attention. One—perhaps his mate, Walton thought—passed near the cabin every night, responding to Satan's cries.

His prisoner was somewhat of a ventriloquist, he wrote, noting that his animal cries seemed to come from the sky, when he was actually on the ground a few feet away. One moonlit night, a friend from town joined Walton to listen to the far-flung sounds. The visitor's attention was momentarily diverted from Satan staked in the dooryard when the first cry pierced the night air. Startled, the man snapped his head to gaze up into the trees overhead, thinking that was the source of the wail. Only when he watched closely as Satan, sitting on his haunches, head thrust up with his nose pointing skyward, blew the sound out between his half-closed lips, was he ready to agree with Walton that the raccoon did, indeed, seem to be throwing his voice off into the distance.

The friend had brought a blanket and hammock and was prepared to spend the night in the open air. Slinging his bed between two nearby trees, he and Walton turned in about 10 o'clock. But the man was nervous and restless; every fifteen or twenty minutes he questioned his host about some noise in the night. About midnight a stoat dropped onto his blanket.

"There was a smothered cry, full of fear, and a flying figure that did not stop until it reached my hammock," an amused Walton wrote later. "Nothing that I could say would induce the frightened man to go back to bed."

Deciding he'd sleep better in the cabin, the city dweller crawled into the bunk, pulling his blanket up over him. What he didn't know, but Walton did, was that the cabin was overrun with white-footed mice. In his hammock, an amused Walton listened quietly for the trouble he knew was sure to come.

Twenty minutes later he heard several war-whoops and saw his friend tumble out of the cabin into the dooryard. Although he tried to assure him that the mice were harmless, the man was panic-stricken.

"I sleep with my mouth open," he cried. "Suppose one of those mice had run down my throat and choked me to death? I'm going home."

After accompanying his distraught guest through the woods to Western Avenue, Walton returned in time to get a few hours' sleep before daybreak. His friend, he thought, was like hundreds of other nervous people he'd known who were too squeamish to enjoy a night in the open air. To be in touch with nature, he felt, one should get accustomed to the presence of a snake in his bed now and then.

In studying the intelligence of the wild masked creature in his dooryard, Walton taught him to pull in his chain, hand over hand, sailor-like. He did this by tying a nut in the twelve-foot chain at a position about two feet from his collar strap. He would then direct Satan to, "Pull in the chain. Pull in the chain." Using his forefeet as hands, the raccoon pulled in the chain to retrieve the nut. Within a week, the nut was removed and he responded to the command without the enticement of food.

"I think he enjoyed the sport," Walton told his journal.

The boys who stopped by the hut thought it was great fun to play with Satan. They'd pull the chain out and watch him pull it in. When Satan tired, he coiled the chain and lay on it, indicating that play was over for the time being. While he was resting, if one of the boys attempted to pull the chain, he'd draw his ears straight back, bare his teeth and growl menacingly. After resting a bit, his manner changed dramatically and he was ready to resume play. This he made known by sitting up on his hind feet, pricking his ears forward and, according to Walton, "look clever." Only then were the boys allowed to reach under him and pull the chain out without danger.

Satan acquired his name because of an incident his captor described as "cruel and crafty." One day while chained to the stake, he killed Walton's pet catbird. Walton had placed a piece of matting by the stake which the coon used as both dining table and bed. One evening after Satan's feeding, a few pieces of cookie remained on the mat. Eyeing the morsels from a nearby tree limb, the bird flew down to help himself. Walton was at his writing desk—an upturned orange crate—under a pine tree about thirty feet away. Glancing up, he caught the flash of Satan's paw and rushed to the bird's rescue. When he reached Satan, the bird was nowhere in sight and Walton assumed he had escaped. He returned to his writing and Satan settled down for a nap.

An hour later a friend from the city stopped by to borrow a rare edition on birds. Walton went into the cabin for the book and when he returned, Satan was patting down the edge of the mat.

"When he saw me, he put on his innocent look and coiled up as if he were going to sleep in a different spot," wrote his keeper. "My suspicion was aroused. I pulled him away and under the mat found the dead bird. He had killed it and placed it under him so swiftly that I didn't detect the trick when I rushed to the rescue."

For a full hour the rascal feigned sleep with the dead bird under him. When Walton went to the cabin, he quickly hid his prey under the mat. His punishment was a severe whipping. The next day Walton buried his little pet under a pine tree a short distance away so Satan would not benefit from his deed. The coon remembered the whipping and never molested birds again—at least not in the hermit's presence. Once a young towhee bunting sat on his hind foot and ate a piece of cookie that Satan tried to hide. Walton watched as the bird ate his fill and flew away from a motionless Satan. He wondered how the little bird would have fared if he hadn't been close by.

One day in late June Walton joined the throngs of spectators lining Main Street to watch the parade of the big, three-ring Barnum Circus that arrived in town that morning. The loud, clapping sounds of animal hoofs striking the granite roadway filled the air as gaily-decorated camels, horses, elephants and caged lions rolled past.

After the parade he joined the excited crowd making its way along Western Avenue to Stage Fort Park for performances under the Big Top. As he was more interested in viewing the exotic wildlife than watching the aerial acts, Walton headed for the animal tent. In front of a cage containing two lions, he noticed a rather unusual-looking individual acting strangely. The man wore a cowboy hat, black and white checkered coat, red vest and purple pants. From a distance, Walton silently observed as the fellow tried to "stare the lions down." As he watched, a big African male became uneasy under the man's fixed gaze and slunk behind his mate.

"See him cower and hide," he cried, addressing Walton. "The human eye, intelligently used, can subdue the most ferocious brute living. I could enter that cage and handle those lions like kittens."

Walton didn't dispute his boast. When the stranger asked if there were any wild animals in the woods around Gloucester, he told him about Satan. With a haughty air, the self-styled hypnotist bragged that he could easily train the untamed creature into total submission and asked directions to the cabin.

The next morning, wearing the same gaudy outfit, the man presented himself at the cabin door, self-confident and ready to begin his demonstration. Walton could control Satan whenever or however he pleased, but it was dangerous for a stranger to attempt to touch him. A person could almost step on him without upsetting him, but he drew the line at being man-handled. The flamboyant visitor, whom Walton considered "a dude," fixed his gaze on Satan and slowly approached him, stamping his feet and commanding "Down, Sir! Down, Sir!"

Satan looked at the intruder quizzically, then at Walton, as if to ask, "What's this all about?"

When Walton remained silent, the coon decided to act for himself. With a savage snarl, he sprang at the man, digging his claws into the leg of his purple trousers. Startled and frightened, the would-be animal trainer jumped back beyond the length of Satan's chain, but Satan held on, tearing his pants from hip to knee. Fortunately, his claws did not reach the flesh. Walton repaired the damage, after which the dude, nursing his deflated ego, raced down the hill without so much as a thank you.

With the onset of cold weather, Satan was allowed to winter in the cabin. Placing a box inside and his cage outside, Walton connected the two with boards and a swinging panel. He expected he'd have to teach his wild friend how to operate the passage way, but found it unnecessary. From the cage, Satan pushed at the door flap with his two front paws and entered the box inside. After looking around the new enclosure, he pushed the panel in the opposite direction and jumped out to his cage. Deciding it was great fun, he scampered back and forth, in and out, until he tired of the game.

With the first heavy snowfall, Walton decided it was time to settle in for the winter. In the evening, Satan's chain and collar were removed, giving him the freedom of the cabin. During the night, he was placed in the box. Within a week, Walton felt the animal knew the contents of the cabin as well as he did. In studying Satan's behavior inside the cabin, he noted that the light seemed to puzzle his furry friend. He watched transfixed as Walton lit the lamp, blew it out and relit it. Once—and only once—he touched the chimney of the lamp. His curiosity satisfied, he never attempted to do so again.

One night about midnight Walton was awakened by a touch on his face. Remaining still, he again felt a soft, cold touch on his cheek. With a swift grab, he had Satan by one paw, holding him until he lit the lamp. In the glow he looked into the startled eyes of his captive, which seemed to say innocently, "I didn't mean any harm. I simply wanted to know if you were asleep or dead." When Walton released him, he scurried back to his box, raised the cover himself and settled down for the night.

Life in captivity came to an end for the wild animal several weeks later. When Walton left for the city that morning, he neglected to secure the cage and upon his return, found the door open and Satan gone. The next day he took food to the den under the boulders, but the fugitive was not interested. He was wise to the tricks of man—and he was fat. Retreating into hibernation, he was not seen again until the following spring. In early April his masked face appeared at the mouth of the den and when Walton offered him food, he took it from his hand but kept up his guard to prevent recapture. Walton intended to build a box trap to catch him, but time ran out before he could get to it. When he heard that a farmer had killed a raccoon in his hen-house, he knew Satan had sacrificed his life to his appetite.

Writing about Satan's mental capabilities, he said, "The reckless act did not indicate a lack of reason. Human beings sacrifice their lives to appetite, so which of us will throw the first stone at Satan?"

This trio of forest drummers brought Walton much pleasure.

Chapter 7
Handsome Little Fellows

Walton's study of the natural world in Ravenswood Forest included the white-footed mouse, which he described as "a handsome fellow, sporting a chestnut coat, white vest, reddish brown trousers and white stockings." Like the deer mouse, with which it is often confused, he noted, its eyes and ears are uncommonly large, resembling a deer's head in miniature.

He was intrigued by the unusual communication practice of these little woodland creatures. During fifteen years summering and wintering with them at Ravenswood, he had never, ever, heard one utter a vocal sound. Instead, they sent messages to each other by drumming their toes, holding their forefeet rigid while pounding the toes vigorously. The messages seemed to be coded by the sequence and length of each roll, not its intensity.

The discovery of this fancy footwork was news to Walton. In writing about it in his book, *A Hermit's Wild Friends*, he said, "If any writer has called attention to this peculiar method of communication, it has escaped my reading. I am well satisfied that the habit has never been published before."

As a result of his extensive research, Walton determined that white-footed mice were totally mute. In making this judgment, for some time he had observed a number of them "talking with their toes," much like physically-impaired humans using sign language. When he first noticed this strange behavior, he attempted to interpret their drum rolls by relating them to action and reaction. He found the pattern used time and again to attract attention was a long, drawn-out roll, a call Walton likened to a greeting on the telephone. The response to this from the colony was always the same—silence and attentiveness—after which different rolls delivered messages or issued commands. The danger call was two long, frantic rolls. The food call was a long roll followed by sharp, short rolls. Many times the drummers carried on conversations among themselves, pounding intermittently in give-and-take "muted chatter."

During the winter months Walton provided food and shelter for the animals under study in order to continue his observation. He placed a loaf of bread on the floor of the cabin each evening, enticing about a dozen hungry mice out of their nests to nibble away. When they became hungry again, they scampered out and, in unison, summoned their care-giver for another treat by drumming the long, attention-getting roll. When Walton looked up in response, the pounding changed, with all toes—again in unison—drumming the food call. After a few months of this, they included two short rolls which—after trial and error—he interpreted as a request for water.

In observing the behavior of a female mouse which had become a long-time pet, he noticed her habit of leading her young to the roof of the cabin on cool evenings. The roof was warm which, according to Walton, "made an ideal playground for the little ones." Soon after the mice appeared on the roof, the mother dashed down to the cabin in search of nourishment. When she found it, she summoned her brood with three drum rolls—one long between two short. The young mice then joined her for supper, after which they returned to the roof where they raced and romped until daylight when she put them to bed for the day.

As he studied the communication skills of the mice, Walton took many detailed notes. Among other things, he was impressed by the degree of intelligence exhibited by the young as they grew older. For example, when the female mouse attempted to get Walton's attention for food or water while she was in the cabin, she was ignored by the young mice on the roof. Did they understand she was "talking" to Walton and not to them? Surely they heard her loud, clear drumming just as Walton did, but they paid no attention until the pattern changed to one that summoned them down to their evening meal.

It was Walton's belief that young mice themselves learned to drum when nearly full-grown, but they understood and responded to the drumming of the mother much earlier. Writing in his journal, he noted "I have had proof of this more times than I can remember."

For years three particular female mice lived about his cabin, in time becoming pets. He found them to be smart enough to know that he would protect them from harm. As his friend Frank Bolles wrote of his special bond with forest wildlife, he had become one of their own kind. At times during the night when the mice became upset by some noise, they dove into his bed for reassurance. During the day when they were frightened, they sounded the danger-call, knowing he would respond and drive away a threatening predator.

To a stranger these mice might look as much alike as three peas in a pod, but to Walton their characteristics and behavioral patterns were as different as those of people he knew. For instance, the one that used the roof for a playground always nested under a stone wall in back of the cabin. A second took up lodging in the cabin throughout the year—in warm weather on a high shelf, and on the floor under a pile of newspapers during the winter. The third stayed close to Walton wherever he slept. During the winter months when his bed was the small cot in the cabin, she settled down in various places nearby. When he slept in the open air under his canopied hammock, she followed him, curling up under newspapers or in a box which he set out for her. If she had a family during this transition, it did not seem to matter; she simply made a nest suitable for all in the new quarters.

In recording the intelligence of these three pets, Walton rated number two as the smartest. One reason was the fierce determination with which she carried out her maternal responsibilities. In the summer her nest was in the cabin on a shelf above the bookcase. But when the stove became too hot during the winter, she moved her young to a safer location, knowing they would perish in the extreme heat. Every time Walton filled the stove with wood, she understood what that meant and rushed to the shelf frantically drumming the danger signal. The first time this happened, she drummed furiously in an attempt to make Walton aware of the danger the fire posed for her young, but he did not understand. Realizing this, she feverishly worked to save her babies by inducing each to cling to a teat and crawling along a log to a place of safety with eight raw, shapeless things clinging to her like grim death. The hole in the wall that opened to the outside was small, causing her to struggle to get her load safely through. Now and then a young mouse dropped off and remained squirming where it fell until she returned to retrieve it.

When the mice were half-grown, they were transported differently. Since they were too big to be dragged or carried by the neck, she doubled them up by turning their heads inward and crossing their legs and tucking them underneath. The result was a round, compact bundle which she grasped securely by the lower end. She first tried to carry them through the wall opening while holding them in her mouth, but when she found the hole too small, she turned around and backed through, dragging her load after her. Watching these tender maternal maneuvers, Walton was convinced more than ever that animals in the wild possess the mental capabilities of logic and reason.

This trio of white-footed mice brought Walton much pleasure, as well as providing important first-hand knowledge of their reasoning powers. Although at times, he found them to be a nuisance. In time his pets were joined by other mice that soon took possession of his cabin, building nests in every nook and corner, even in his hat. For many years the population of these small rodents was kept in check by predators—moles and stoats (often described as a weasel with a black tipped tail). For some reason, the stoats disappeared from the forest—at least from the home range of the mice living near the cabin—and the mice began to return in increasing numbers.

Walton did not mind a few mice for company—in fact, he enjoyed having them around on winter evenings—but he drew the line when they became so numerous that he was forced to eat and sleep with them. In trying to reduce his guest list, however, he found they cleverly avoided the traps he set to ensnare them.

One winter he bought a wire rat-trap with a trencher that tipped, sliding its victim into the space below. This, too, failed. The mice found the contraption great fun, using the trencher as a door to run into and out of the enclosure. Not to be outsmarted, Walton attached a wire to the trencher in a way he felt was fool-proof, and it was. Luring the mice into the trap with food, he pulled the wire, imprisoning them inside. The following morning his captives numbered twenty-eight. His plan was to drown the entire lot until he noticed the wild eyes of several pets clinging to the upper wires of the trap. His heart softened and he decided it would be more humane to release them in the woods.

Toting them nearly a mile from the cabin, he turned them loose near some large boulders, leaving a supply of food and a promise that he would return to feed them from time to time. But the mice had other ideas. Two nights later they were all back in the cabin. Upon investigation Walton discovered they had followed his footsteps; he could see their tracks in the snow where they had trooped along in short runs. At the end of each stretch, the tracks disappeared under a boulder or a tree, only to appear again, always heading in the direction of the cabin.

Again Walton baited and set the trap while the mice scampered about celebrating their return. He told them plainly that this would be their last night on earth; that he had outwitted them once and would so again. But his boasting came to naught. Not a single mouse entered the trap while the wire was on the trencher. The third night he removed the wire and the mice, noticing the difference, entered the trap without fear. Walton thought: man had pitted his wit against that of these tiny woodfolk—and they had triumphed. Like sportsmen everywhere, he realized that wild animals could be just as shrewd as humans, and often were.

In his studies of the white-footed mice, Walton joined them in fighting off their natural enemies, namely members of the weasel family, including the stoat, or ermine, and pursued them every month of the year. While rearing their young, by day and night these small carnivorous mammals are a constant threat to the tiny, defenseless mice. Some of the older rats—the more experienced and skillful—escape danger, but not the young. Walton often saw a stoat running along the wall back of his cabin with a mouse in its mouth. It carried its prey by the middle, reminding him of the way tigers carried their human Hottentot victims in South Africa. An auger-hole in one of the logs inside the cabin afforded a safe retreat for a hotly-pursued mouse. Several times Walton watched a stoat thrust its paw into the hole only to jerk it out with a painful yelp. A drop of blood on the log showed that the terrified mouse had defended itself with its sharp teeth.

At one time the little cabin was haunted by a strange sound, a sharp click repeated over and over again. For six weeks Walton searched for the source of the noise which became increasingly annoying, as it interrupted his train of thought when he read or wrote. Finally, he traced it to an empty cigar box in the back of a high shelf where a dozen small mice had retreated from their enemy. When they entered or left the box, they raised the lid and when it fell back into place, it resulted in the annoying clicking sound. The lid was heavy enough to severely pinch a mouse's tail. Once again, displaying their remarkable ability to resolve problems logically, they engineered a channel by gnawing a small hole the size of a lead pencil in the side of the box just below the cover, allowing them to pass in and out without crushing their tails.

For fifteen years Walton recorded the activities of these little white-footed creatures, some comical, others pathetic and still others tragic. An amusing incident occurred when Walton received a visit from a young man from the city seeking to commune with nature. He asked if he could stay one moonlight evening to watch the mice eat. As often happened when the mice gathered around their loaf of bread, a star-nosed mole would appear and scatter them in all directions. If Walton were nearby, it was not unusual for one of them to run up his trousers leg.

Perhaps it was his Down East sense of humor that prompted him to allow his guest the chair near the woodfolk's banquet table because what he expected to happen, did. The mole made his appearance, sending the panicky mice helter-skelter, one of which dashed up his visitor's leg.

"With a war-whoop that would have frightened an Indian, he bounded into the dooryard, but the mouse escaped from beneath his coat collar before he got out of the cabin," wrote the mischievous Walton later. "The young man danced around like a crazy man. Whenever his clothes touched him, he thought the mouse was on the attack and slapped himself so hard that he must have raised blisters. When I could control my laughter, I told him that the mouse had escaped, but I couldn't get him to enter the cabin again."

In examining nests made by the mice throughout the years, Walton found most to be round in shape using materials gathered from their surroundings. Near the cabin, for instance, they were made of bits of paper matted with cotton batting and soft wool from his old clothes. Those farther away, usually found in a tangle of catbrier, were constructed of dried leaves, grasses and plant-down. The nests were occupied during the winter and were cleverly designed to be rain and frost proof. Walton also found nests in discarded tin cans and paper bags left by picnickers.

Walton noted the mothers of this species of mice are devoted to the care of their young which are born blind and naked. While small they're raw-looking things, but wiry, tough and tenacious. At this stage full-grown moles would destroy a family in a few seconds if it were not for the mother's watchful eye.

As the young mice grow, their coats change to a dark lead color which they retain until the first moult, he reported. Their diet consists of insects, berries, seeds, nuts and—thanks to him—those around the cabin enjoyed bread, cheese and all kinds of meat. They're fond of mushrooms and never, like some humans, eat the poisonous varieties. Their food for winter is usually stored in holes in the ground and hollow trees and logs. Walton's guests stored food in anything they could. Once he found a shoe half full of nuts and corn.

In summing up his research on these wild friends, he wrote in his journal, "The white-footed mouse makes an interesting study, affording me many proofs of its intelligence."

Chapter 8
A Little Rogue

On returning to his cabin one sunny October afternoon, Walton found a young male song-sparrow in his dooryard, bleeding from a shot in the muscle of a wing joint. Despite the bird's violent struggle to free himself, he administered first aid, after which his feathered patient hopped into the bushes and hid.

"I think he held a poor opinion of my surgical skill," noted the attending physician in his record book.

The next day, the little bird joined others fluttering about the dooryard. Because his flight faltered and, in Walton's eyes, took on "a peculiar wabble," he decided to name him "Wabbles." With the approach of cold weather, the song-sparrows in Ravenswood joined others on Cape Ann in migrating southward, leaving the injured bird behind. Walton expected him to remain cabin-bound during the winter, but one day he awoke to find his guest missing.

On a blustery March morning, he looked out upon the snow banks and saw his little feathered friend in the dooryard. Walton did not know where the bird had wintered but evidently he remembered the little log cabin in the woods and understood that food and a welcome awaited him, which they did. When the other birds returned that spring, they lingered about the cabin for about a month and then scattered to neighboring fields and pastures which sparrows normally prefer to dark woodlands. Since Wabbles' wing joint was still tender, he again remained behind when the others flew off for the mating season. While they were gone, Walton enjoyed a special kinship with "the little rogue," as he affectionately called him, bonding a friendship that would last for many years.

Each morning at daybreak, Walton was awakened by a natural alarm clock. Hopping about in the bushes near the hammock, the pretty little songbird began with low, nasal calls, followed by three or four bright, musical trills. He usually sang only in the morning, but when Walton returned after a long absence, he burst into a lively expression of joy, no matter the time of day. That fall he was strong enough to migrate with the rest of the sparrows, leaving Walton to wonder about him for the next few months.

The mystery of animal migration posed a number of questions for Walton, as the Ravenswood forest fell silent under blankets of winter snow. He wondered now, as he had when he was a boy in Maine, why birds migrate south when food was still available in the North and why they leave the South when food is available there year round. He questioned how their flights are directed since many small birds fly at night, some over hundreds of miles of water. His notes on the subject were most interesting.

From the beginning of such studies, ornithologists and other scientists have been challenged by the principles of biophysics in relation to the annual ritual of bird migration. Like the uninformed, experts are astonished by the extremes to which some birds migrate. Flight records obtained by banding reveal many fascinating adventures by these small, feathered, flying machines.

In examining records of birds migrating to and from New England, Walton studied the flight of a barn swallow weighing only fifteen grams (about half an ounce) banded in Massachusetts on June 28. On August 26 of the same year, it was found dead in Florida—a distance of 1,225 miles.

Another record he found was that of a purple finch banded in Central Massachusetts and recovered in Bar Harbor, Maine three days later. This small bird, related to the sparrow family, flies at speeds between twenty to thirty miles an hour.

A third study showed that a medium-sized sandpiper traveled from the coast of Massachusetts to the Panama Canal Zone, averaging 125 miles a day for the 2,300-mile flight. Another sandpiper flew 2,400 miles from Massachusetts to Venezuela in twenty-six days, averaging ninety-two miles a day.

These figures are all the more amazing when one realizes that the flights of these birds are maintained solely by the work of living muscle. They store up fat before their long journey and are fueled during flight by catching and digesting food along the way.

Most experts theorize that the routes followed by migrating birds are governed by their own internal nervous systems, guiding them northward in spring and south in the fall. Others attribute their directional finders to celestial bodies, polarized light and magnetic fields.

Worth mentioning is the fact that, during the early stages of radar detection, migrating flocks appeared as small "blips" on radar screens. But since they were not metallic, they posed no threat and were not challenged by the military—which categorized them as harmless "angels."

As to why and when birds migrate north for the breeding season, this essentially takes place during an annual cycle when birds become physiologically ready for reproduction. Their ovaries and testes increase in size ten fold, they become interested in the opposite sex and begin to search for suitable nesting sites, establishing territories from which other males are chased away. Songs, too, play a role in the mating game, as does appearance. The plumage of most, but not all, males changes to bright, vibrant colors.

Walton found that the theories advanced by experts on the subject of animal and bird migration are many and varied. They ranged from the aerodynamics of speed by the mouse-eared bat to the seasonal flights of monarch butterflies, from the orientation of salmon by the sun to the various migratory movements of reindeer. To him, migration was one of nature's most fascinating phenomena, and he recommended several excellent books on the subject to readers of a newspaper article he wrote.

Notes concerning Wabbles indicate that, during spring migration of the second year, the little song sparrow returned to Ravenswood from the rice fields of Louisiana two weeks ahead of the others. He stayed about the hermit's cabin until the mating season and then disappeared for five days, returning with "a shy, demure little wife."

Walton made copious notes of the lovebirds' activities, which later became the basis for a tender story in his book, *A Hermit's Wild Friends*. He wrote about their nesting site (she preferred the open fields, he the forest near the cabin), their first brood ("from four dainty, speckled eggs emerged three baby sparrows") and Wabbles' overnight visit to the cabin with his young, ("putting them to bed on a twig, concealed by a spray of hemlock").

"When I approached, three little heads turned and six bright eyes looked at me, but they showed no sign of fear," he told his readers of their social call.

The sparrow's mate, whom Walton called "Mrs. Wabbles" throughout the story, disapproved of her spouse's little adventure and chirped loudly her displeasure.

"Undoubtedly, she gave him a piece of her mind for taking her babies to the woods," he wrote, resigning himself to the fact that "his friend, Wabbles, the warrior, was henpecked." But in time she, too, succumbed to the old man's charm, and was soon eating from his outstretched hand.

One spring Wabbles returned from migration on the 10th of March, bringing with him a male linnet, three weeks before the latter's usual arrival. A week later Wabbles' mate returned with the linnet's mate, confirming Walton's view that birds and animals possess feelings, thoughts and intelligence. The birds evidently met in the South and made plans to spend the summer together on Cape Ann.

"It proved that two species of the bird family can communicate ideas to each other," he noted.

In late fall, death claimed the life of the female sparrow, shot by a boy from the city. Wabbles was not the only one to mourn her loss, as Walton had become attached to her also and was saddened by the tragedy.

"Wabbles lost his joyfulness," he wrote. "He watched over his motherless babies with great care but did not sing for a long time."

The following spring when Wabbles returned to the forest, his young did not accompany him, nor did they return later. Walton speculated that perhaps some motherly bird had adopted them, taking them into the fields or pastures. After several weeks, Wabbles disappeared for three days. When he returned, he brought along another mate, an "old bird, probably a widow," noted Walton.

In his book, Walton told his readers that the songbird set up a singing school and trained his young to sing the mating song of his species. In the preface he wrote, "I am aware that some of my claims will be vigorously assailed, but I have verified these discoveries by years of patient observation." The singing school theory was among those later challenged by his critics.

Wabbles was familiar to summer visitors. The story of the little sparrow that deserted the fields for life in the forest was known in town, and people came to see for themselves. He seemed to enjoy the attention showered on him but, like some domestic pets, was jealous when other birds became too friendly with the hermit.

"He firmly believes that he holds a mortgage on the dooryard," Walton told callers.

Some considered the little fellow a tyrant, a view Walton did not share. He knew the songster better than anyone and felt that, although fiery on occasion, he was also intelligent and, at times, caring and kind. To illustrate his point, he told critics about finding a severely-injured chickadee in the dooryard whose leg had been destroyed by gunshot. Wabbles hopped around him all day, chirping gentle, soothing notes. Up to the time of winter migration, the little chickadee was allowed the freedom—and the food—of the dooryard with Wabbles' blessing.

In addition to the hermit, Wabbles had another ardent admirer in the person of Mrs. William Russell, wife of the Governor of Massachusetts.

"She's quite fond of him," Walton once told a reporter. "After mealtime, he flies up into a hemlock tree and sings for us. The song is sweeter and lower in tone than the mating song."

Mrs. Russell met the Ravenswood resident during summer visits to Magnolia with her family. An avid bird watcher, she was pleased at the many species she saw and heard during walks through the park and often asked Walton to identify them. The governor also found pleasure in the man described as "the philosophical fellow who made Ravenswood famous." On many occasions, they tramped the dark woods together, exploring the mysteries of nature and discussing important political issues of the day.

It had been fourteen years since Walton performed surgery on his wing when the story of Wabbles appeared in *A Hermit's Wild Friends* in 1903.

"Dear old Wabbles," Walton wrote lovingly of his avian friend. "He has blessed me with a friendship as sincere and lasting as any that can spring from the human heart. As years go by, I am more and more impressed with the little bird's individuality and his sense of morality."

It appears their unique friendship continued for many more years. In 1915, twelve years after he penned those words, he was interviewed by a reporter from the *Boston Globe* who asked about Wabbles.

Walton told him that the little songbird he found bleeding in his dooryard twenty-six years earlier, at the time had his second year feathers. It would seem from this that Wabbles lived to be at least twenty-eight years old, which is extremely unusual. Song sparrows held in captivity are known to live much longer than those in the wild, some even to the age reported by Walton. But the lifespan of birds left to fend for themselves is much shorter. Could it be that the love and care the hermit provided Wabbles for so many years prolonged the little fellow's life to such an extent?

Chapter 9
Other Feathered Friends

The object of Walton's attention on Thursday morning, May 27, 1886 was a young, female chestnut-sided warbler which he easily recognized by its pretty yellow crown and chestnut sides.

He looked on with amusement as the little bird pranced about the dooryard in graceful, mincing steps. In a box beside the cabin, he kept remnants of string, fabric, cotton, paper and plant down—and when he found them, snake skins—for use by birds in building their nests.

Discovering the cache for the first time, the little warbler seemed to understand its purpose and responded in kind to the pleasant storekeeper. After the first year, she allowed him to sit by her nests from the time the first blade of grass was laid until her young were ready to fly. During their friendship, which lasted eleven years, he recorded the construction of thirteen nests, two of which were robbed by snakes and replaced. None was alike, and all except two were saddled on the forks of small bushes. Scientific writings to the contrary, Walton noted that one was pensile, hanging between two shoots of a currant bush without benefit of support at the bottom.

As with all wildlife under his scrutiny, he took careful note of the significant events in the little warbler's life, including seasonal migrations, nesting and family activities.

On May 27, 1902, exactly six years to the day of her first visit, the same friendly, little warbler hopped to Walton's feet, once again in search of nesting materials. After greeting her warmly, he placed several eight-inch pieces of cotton twine on his knee. Picking up two strands, she flew to a sweetpepper bush in a hollow near his spring. Walton followed and seated himself on a nearby boulder to observe her actions. From time to time he reached out and touched the nest and was completely ignored by the busy little worker. But when he placed grass or string on his knee, her sharp eyesight discovered it immediately and, after close inspection, she carried it to her building site.

For seven days Walton watched as the small bird, with the help of her mate, gathered materials from the box and worked diligently to lodge the nest securely between the main stem and two twigs of the bush. On the last day she spent most of the time shaping its interior by pressing the walls with her muddy breast, the outer edges having been loosely woven with her beak during construction. When finished it was firmly compacted and as round as an apple.

Examining it closely, Walton smiled to himself when he recognized shreds of gray wool from an old coat he had discarded.

In early June the cozy nursery contained four cream-colored eggs tinged with reddish-brown and lilac. After they hatched, the bird-lover decided to train the young birdlings to respond to his call. He had sat beside the mother through the birth and rearing of a number of broods and felt he had gained her trust.

To nourish the new-born, he bred some meal worms which he gently passed to them despite initial concern by the mother. But after awhile she came to trust him and looked on while he fed her babies from his finger tips. When they were old enough to flutter about in the shrubbery, he called to them but only one responded.

"The others," he noted, "preferred to feed themselves."

When the birds returned to Cape Ann from migration the following spring, he looked for the young warbler he sought to tame but to no avail.

Eleven years passed and—*once again on May 27th*—the matriarch of the warbler family found her way to the cabin dooryard to gather material for yet another nest. During that time, the years had deepened the wrinkles lining the old man's face but, like the venerable Wabbles, this little feathered friend appeared ageless. She was as blithe and gay as she had been on the morning of her first visit.

In the ensuing years, Walton noticed the chestnut-sided warblers that nested along Old Salem Road were quite friendly, often coming within three feet of admirers. It was his opinion that many were descendants of the docile little mother bird that visited his storehouse each May. [For some reason, this little bird remained nameless despite their long, loving relationship.]

Black-capped chickadees were year-round visitors to Walton's cabin retreat. Easily identified by their deep black crown and hindneck, these "small boys of winter" were always in fine spirits, he noted. They seemed to actually enjoy snowstorms. Like nuthatches and kinglets, their frequent companions, they were seen frolicking from tree to tree during the harsh New England weather.

In the wintertime those inhabiting the Ravenswood forest gathered into a flock and remained near the cabin, depending on Walton for food. When the snow melted they drifted off in pairs in search of nesting sites—in due time bringing back their young for treats. After a meal of flying, crawling and jumping insects, they knew they'd find dessert in the dooryard.

"It is a rare treat to watch a pair of chickadees in the nesting season,"

Walton wrote. "Their domestic life overflows with love, joy and devotion."

Just such a pleasure began on a morning bright with sunshine as Walton walked back from the city. Turning up Old Salem Road, he heard a clear *dee-dee-dee* from a nearby beech tree. It was the call of a female which had won his affection several seasons earlier. Whenever she met him in the woods, she'd call in a variety of high-pitched sounds, garbled notes and sputters and then sound her sweet, tender *dee-dee-dee.*

On this day his pert, little friend flew to his shoulder to nibble at the donut he offered. When she'd had her fill, she flew down the side hill to Magnolia Swamp and, as was his practice, Walton followed. There in the cavity of a small, dead paper birch, her mate was hard at work building a nest. He was easily persuaded to take a break when given the remainder of the donut. Attacking it vigorously, he then flew into a patch of hempweed vines and finished off his breakfast with a few seeds.

"I talk to the chickadees as I would to human beings," wrote Walton in his book about his wild friends. "So I told them I was making a friendly call and begged them to keep right on with their work."

Seating himself on a boulder, he watched as the lovebirds worked together on their new home. Methodically they chipped away with their short, sharp bills to enlarge and deepen the hole in the birch. First the male hammered at the bottom and the female, clinging to the edge of the hole, reached down inside to bring out a beak-full of tiny bits. At intervals they changed places and she pounded away while he disposed of the wood chips. From time to time Walton visited the nest to inspect their work. When the hole was about nine inches in depth, they began to add building material.

"If they had not become partly domesticated," he noted, "the foundation would have been moss and leaves with a lining of fur or grouse feathers. My chickadees used cotton-batting for the foundation and lining."

Eight small eggs soon appeared in the nest. These were very similar in color and pattern to those of the warbler, white spotted with chestnut and purplish-gray. All birdlings arrived safely.

Walton estimated the flock of chickadees around the cabin during the winter months numbered about fifty. They had become so tame they entered the cabin and ate from his dinner table.

One female in particular showed remarkable intelligence and memory. For four winters she adopted a routine of pecking at the small side window of the cabin when she was hungry. Then she flew to the front door to be admitted. If

Walton didn't respond, she returned to the window and repeated the summons with loud, persistent raps until she was heard. Walton marveled at her ability to think logically. She knew a) there was food in the cabin, b) she was allowed to eat it, c) the way to get in was through the door, and d) to get his attention to open it, she had to knock at the window—and all these maneuvers she recalled from one winter to another!

Walton enjoyed telling stories of wildlife intelligence to friends. But when he boasted that one of his chickadees could count to four, Frank Bolles was not convinced. The pragmatic Bolles was Secretary of Harvard College and the author of several books on outdoor life. He wanted proof.

"I am quite a bird crank," he laughed. "But I think I will have to draw the line at counting,"

To prove his point, Walton offered a handful of hemp seeds to one of his older female pets. The bird took four and flew to a nearby tree, depositing three on a branch near its trunk and taking the fourth to a small twig about eight feet away. Holding the seed between her toes, she beat off the hull to get at the meat. While she was doing so, Walton pushed one of the three seeds off the branch onto the ground. Looking on, Bolles voiced the opinion that she wouldn't miss it. He was wrong.

After eating three, the little bird poked around in the bark of the tree for the fourth, then dropped to the ground and searched until she found it. Returning to the limb, she removed the hull in the same manner as before and ate the contents.

Then with a proud, "I-told-you-so" gleam in his eyes, Walton carried the demonstration a step further—by pushing off two seeds. The little chickadee performed right on cue, hunting around on the forest floor until she retrieved both grains. The demonstration satisfied the doubting Mr. Bolles.

On one occasion, Bolles visited Walton and found he was not at home. It was a warm, sunny day and he decided to stretch out in the hammock and await his friend's return. Presently two chickadees approached a box of birdseed the hermit had nailed to a pine limb. From the swamp a pair of catbirds appeared and fed upon a few crumbs in the dooryard as a chipmunk ran back and forth past them within reach of Bolles' hand. Soon Wabbles appeared and drove away the catbirds. This pleasant woodland scenario depicting wildlife living in harmony with man must have been on the scholar's mind when he later wrote that his friend was "no longer a man, but a faun...one of their own kind."

While Walton's views on animal intelligence conflicted at times with those of the eminent naturalist, John Burroughs, the two were in solid agreement about one characteristic of chickadees. They were amusing little tricksters.

Burroughs' example appeared in the National Audubon Society's *Birds of America*, for which he was consulting editor. It concerned a protective mother sitting on her nest in the hollow of a small sassafras tree. When several college girls drew close and looked down at her, she resented the intrusion upon her privacy. As one was taking a long peek, there was a faint explosion at the bottom of the cavity and the startled girl jerked her head back and cried, "Why, it spit at me!"

"The trick of this little bird on such occasions," wrote Mr. Burroughs, "is apparently to draw in its breath till its form swells and then give forth a quick, explosive sound like an escaping jet of steam. Anyone close by involuntarily closes his eyes and jerks back his head."

This deceptive trait by these tiny charmers was corroborated by Walton's findings. Writing about them in his book, he said they were "like a lot of children turned out of school" when he placed a box of birdseed out for them in the dooryard.

He recorded several occasions during which a tree-sparrow appeared and drove all the other birds away.

"That's when the chickadees mobilized into action. One sounded the danger call, sending the tree-sparrow darting into the bushes and the chickadees piling onto the seed-box. Seeing no enemy about, the sparrow returned to the seed-box, scattering the chickadees in all directions. Shortly another chickadee gave the alarm, again sending the sparrow into the shrubbery. By then he realized he'd been tricked. When he came back the third time, he chased the chickadees through the trees but never caught them.

"The chickadees were too quick for the sparrow, darting this way and that, laughing and shouting at the top of their voices," wrote the amused journalist.

As is true with people, there was sorrow in the lives of these pretty little birds.

Once Walton placed a small box in the top of an oak tree, hoping to draw the beautiful blue-coated, gentle-mannered bluebird to the Ravenswood aviary. The next day when he returned from the city, he found it occupied by a pair of chickadees busily carrying cotton batting to the site. Later, during the incubation period, he climbed the tree every day to offer food to the mother-to-be.

One day about noontime he found eight raw, little birdlings and noted that "the parents appeared brimful of joy and happiness." He visited the nest daily to check on them, at times bringing insects and worms, at others soft bread crumbs. As he watched their development, he looked forward to seeing them wing through the forest with their parents. Then tragedy struck. His journal told the sad story.

"When the young birds were full grown, I took one in my hand and the mother said something to me in her language. I thought she asked me if the bird was old enough to leave the nest. I told her it was and the sooner they all got out the better, for the nest was too small and was hot besides.

"That noon I went over to Cedar Swamp and did not return until after sunset. When I had reached the cabin, the chickadees hopped to my shoulder and in heart-rending bird language tried to tell me that something had happened to their babies. I climbed the tree and found the nest empty.

"On a boulder I had placed a pair of rubber boots to dry. One of the boots was missing. Two boys had robbed the chickadees and carried away the young birds in the rubber boot. The bereaved parents remained near the cabin all night and I did not sleep because they talked to me in the most pitiful language I had ever heard from a bird. The next day I traced the wretched thieves, but the little birds were dead."

At half-past five on a clear, warm May morning, Walton sat at breakfast beneath an ancient hemlock reading Thoreau's *Maine Woods*. The plain-living woods-man considered his breakfast under the conifers a "grand affair," but he dropped the custom later in favor of swapping stories with Gloucester fishermen at a Pavilion Beach coffeehouse.

Ravenswood in springtime literally bursts with music from the forest's feath-ered flock. Raising their voices to greet each new day was an exuberant chorus of whistlers, mimics, chippers, trillers, high-pitchers, name-sayers, songsters and woodpeckers.

This morning, as Walton sipped coffee and read about Thoreau's visit to a bateau manufactory in his native Old Town, the musicians included three veer-ies, a song sparrow, a robin, a chewink, a catbird, two wood thrushes and a chestnut-sided warbler. Interrupting their light-hearted melodies was a loud out-burst from a small, slender bird perched on the bough of a nearby hemlock. Hopping to the end of the hermit's bench, she proudly announced herself by name, *chewink*.

Walton suspected that his little visitor had learned about his catering service and had come to establish friendly relations. He tossed her a piece of cookie which rolled to the ground. She hopped down and found the treat, ate it on the

The hermit loved Mrs. Chewink, but didn't think much of her lazy husband.

spot, then looked up for more. The second piece she whisked away into the bushes.

As he ate supper later, she was back again, this time joined by two young males which Walton assumed to be rivals.

"They strutted around with their tails spread out like fans," he wrote, "and cared more about showing their fine clothes than they did about eating."

After their evening meal, the birds took flight. Later he looked them up and found the female perched on a limb while her two admirers continued to prance before her. For three days the ritual continued. On the morning of the fourth day, the little miss made her choice and brought her groom to breakfast in the cabin dooryard. The other suitor disappeared, perhaps to find a second choice.

For two years the newlyweds attempted a family but nest after nest was looted by snakes. In the spring of the third year, they were successful.

"Mrs. Chewink," as Walton affectionately called the female, "was very industrious and worked early and late gathering straw, roots and bits of weedstalk for a nest." But he felt she made the wrong choice for a husband.

"Mr. Chewink turned out to be a lazy, good-for-nothing, shiftless fellow. Not even a feather did he carry to the new home."

When the little ones were out of the shell, the mother had all she could do to supply their needs, carrying bread from the dooryard and gleaning bugs and beetles from the flower garden. And again, no help from her ne'er-do-well spouse.

As he followed the family's progress, Walton became concerned about the tiny birdlings' diet. Mrs. Chewink preferred sweets over bread for herself and never ate bread when cup cakes or other pastries were available. He expected her to feed sweets to her babies and was prepared to remove them if they proved harmful.

He decided to oversee the feeding one morning when both cup cakes and bread were on the menu. Although rain made it difficult for the little mother to gather food from the dooryard, she persevered in her efforts. After gorging herself with the cup cake, she carried some back to her young. Walton followed close behind and when he reached the nest, she was feeding them the last of the sweet. From what he observed, the food was divided evenly.

Returning to the cabin, he found the mother in the dooryard. This time she took bread and each time thereafter during three more trips. On her fourth and fifth visits, she gathered bugs and insects from the flower garden, followed by a sixth visit to the dooryard for cup cake. On her seventh and final trip she selected bread.

While she was at the nest with the last delivery, Walton removed the bread from the dooryard. He wanted to see how much of the cup cake she would feed the babies. When she returned and found the bread gone, she ignored the pastry and flew to the garden for insects. He repeated this test several times and in every instance the babies received only a tiny sampling of the cake. When they were older and stronger, she fed them more.

Walton grew very fond of this little mother bird but his feelings about her mate were less than favorable. The worthless husband did have one redeeming quality, however. He could sing beautifully.

"Somehow his song seemed to fit into the glorious spring mornings. It was in perfect harmony with wild flowers, with the drowsy hum of insect life and the tinkling notes of the woodland brook."

Walton's commentary on the activities of Mr. and Mrs. Chewink revealed that birdlife domesticity is much like that of people. Like many human mothers, Mrs. Chewink was overworked. During the summer, she often sought rest in the hemlock grove. Her open bill and drooping wings told Walton she was suffering from the heat. All the while Mr. Chewink haunted the cool, shady spots, leaving his over-burdened wife to care for the young who soon grew as large as their parents.

One morning Mrs. Chewink brought the fledglings into the dooryard. Walton presumed this meant they were old enough to feed themselves. Certainly it lessened her labors. But as it turned out, she had another reason.

Two weeks later they arrived with Mr. Chewink which aroused great anxiety in Walton who thought his little pet had been killed. Searching for her in the shrubs on the hill, he was relieved to hear her loud *chewink, chewink*. She was gathering material for a new nest. He then understood why she had brought her family to the dooryard.

"She was concerned about putting them under the care of her lazy mate so she brought them to where food was plentiful."

But the young birds did not take kindly to their father's care, Walton learned.

"When they found that he was their sole dependence, they made his life miserable. They followed him with open bills and fluttering wings, clamoring for food, causing him to 'act like a crazy bird.'"

He flew around and gathered food and jabbed it into an open bill, often in his reckless haste knocking a little one off its feet. Walton pitied the poor birds and concluded that birds and humans are much alike.

A young girl who visited the park with her parents one Sunday afternoon watched these activities. Walton told her the birds were Mr. Chewink's babies and she looked on attentively as they clamored around him for food. When he knocked one over in his rough, impatient way, the sympathetic little girl exclaimed, "Oh, mamma, how cross he is! He is just like papa when the baby cries."

As part of this study, Walton reported that two days before the second eggs hatched, the male chewink led his offspring to a pond off Old Salem Road where there was plenty of food and water. Each day he returned to check on them.

"Many birds that rear two broods take the first to such a spot so the mother-bird can feed the second family unmolested," he wrote.

The concept of this "bird resort," as he called it, also came under attack by critics.

As Walton walked by the pond one afternoon, one of the young Chewinks remembered him and followed him back to the cabin. When his less-than-happy father found him in the dooryard, he pecked and beat him. But the little bird remained despite the whippings.

Sadly, a black snake descended on the nest one day, swallowing the new brood. Walton later found the glutton sleeping on a sunny patch of bed-rock and killed it. Although he was very interested in studying the reptile, he was much more interested in protecting the baby birds. The following day the banished birds were brought home.

After the death of her new birdlings, Mrs. Chewink remained about the dooryard most of the time. She gathered berries with the rest of her family and hopped to Walton's dinner table for cup cake when it was offered. Afterward she'd stand on a rock near his writing table and preen her feathers.

Of all the birds that nested near the cabin, this delicate little chewink was among his favorites, perhaps because of the treatment she endured from her abusive husband. Walton liked to have her around, to him she seemed more like a human being than a bird. After the breeding season, old birds shed their feathers and become "sorry-looking objects." Mr. Chewink seemed to hate the site of his wife during this time. He pecked her and did not let her eat until he finished.

One time Walton threw a bit of cookie to her which fell behind a box. While she was eating it, her disagreeable mate called from the bushes then flew into the yard looking for food. Mrs. Chewink left the prized treat and sauntered out from behind the box as if she had been looking for food and found none. She made great pretense of eating dry corn and flour bread, though Walton doubted that she swallowed any of it. Her suspicious husband hopped toward the hidden cookie but seeing his wife in the act of "eating," turned to see what she had. Realizing it was only "common food," he flew at her, pecked her severely then flew away. Mrs. Chewink returned to the spot behind the box and finished her cookie in peace, once again attesting to the reasoning ability of his little feathered friends.

The first of November that year was bright and cold with a hint of winter in the air. The Chewinks lingered around the cabin a while longer and then left for their summer home in the South. The following spring Mrs. Chewink did not return which saddened her Ravenswood man-friend.

"I do not know what became of my little pet," he noted touchingly. "Association with her for three seasons led me to become so attached to her that her loss really gave me a heartache."

When Mr. Chewink did not return the following year, Walton did not mourn. He had tamed him enough to eat from his hand, but was completely put off by his unpleasant disposition.

"He abused his wife and children and was as selfish as a hog," read the closing note in Walton's journal.

One Sunday morning some young boys brought a young English sparrow to the hermit for his special brand of medical treatment. They had found the injured bird near an old barn on the hill above Western Avenue just in time to rescue it from the claws of a prowling cat. Upon examination Walton found that its wings and body were severely damaged and thought there was not much chance of recovery. But in the hope that it might survive, he placed it on a bench across the road from the cabin.

A plan conceived by Walton, but never carried out during his lifetime, was to replace the English sparrows in Boston Common with a flock of chickadees from Ravenswood Park, as it was his opinion that his cheerful little chickadees would make desirable park birds. No doubt he was right, but his goal was never realized.

"Your bird is coming to life," a lady called to Walton one morning from the bench across the road.

As they watched, the little sparrow staggered to his feet, but he was badly crippled. Walton nourished him with crumbs, and he ate heartily which was encouraging to his viewers.

In the early evening he ventured over to the cabin and hobbled up the embankment to a barberry bush where he settled in for the night. The next day he tottered down to the cabin for breakfast, after which Walton gently placed him on a rock beside the brook. For three days the tiny patient followed the same routine—sleeping in the barberry bush at night, staggering down the bank to the cabin for food, then resting on the rock at the water's edge.

On the fourth day while Walton was feeding the recovering sparrow, an old chewink hopped over to the loaf of bread in the dooryard. Seeing the hermit's new guest, the chewink called out but received no response. After awhile the sparrow limped over to see what the chewink wanted and noticed the bread. He helped himself then flew unsteadily into the bushes with the chewink. The next day the sparrow returned alone but the following day the birds arrived and left together.

To his surprise three days later Walton, who knew all his bird friends on sight, saw the sparrow near the old barn on Western Avenue. He was with other sparrows but, upon seeing the hermit, immediately flew to him and ate from his outstretched hand.

"How did the chewink know where to take the sparrow?" he wondered. "Was it charity that returned the lost one to his friends or did he entice him away for selfish purposes?"

Whatever the reason, Walton once again had cause to believe in the intelligence of his little feathered friends.

On a golden Sunday morning in May 1897, Memorial Day to be exact, while church bells called saint and sinner to worship in the city of Gloucester, the mewing, cat-like notes of a catbird and the breezy, downward whistle of a veery called the hermit to do the same. The sights and sounds of the forest took on an ethereal quality as he turned down the path leading to Magnolia Swamp. Plowing through waist-high cinnamon fern, he followed the narrow trail which brought him to his destination—a stand of oaks at the base of a hill which he called "the woodpeckers' sap orchard." For two seasons he had carefully noted the curious way these chisel-billed tree climbers tapped trees and decided to spend a few hours in silent observation to gather more information about them.

The hardwood trees for the most part were covered with fully-developed leaves. As usual the white oaks were late, their leaves tiny and at a distance appeared silvery gray in the morning sunshine. To the west of Magnolia Swamp, the hillsides were lightened by this immature foliage. Interspersed with dark green hemlocks, they blended into the peaceful forest landscape.

Walton found the sap orchard deserted. Many of the canoe birches were dead or dying, their lifeblood drained by the sapsuckers and hummingbirds. All the maples were still standing but many of the gray birches had been broken off by the wind just below the belt of punctures.

During his search for another sap orchard, Walton spied a barred owl winging his way to a grove of small hemlocks. In his bill was a leopard frog, ending his search for breakfast. Dropping to his hands and knees, the philosophical fellow who had become a Ravenswood faun, followed, slowly and quietly, finding the great bird on a low bough.

Walton watched as the owl crushed the bones of the legs and joints of the victimized frog, leisurely preparing to swallow it. Afterward he spent several minutes preening his feathers before settling down for a nap. A pair of cheerful chickadees, also in search of their Sunday breakfast, discovered the owl and sounded the alarm. Within minutes Walton counted thirty six birds, including cuckoos, warblers, blue jays, thrushes, vireos, flycatchers and buntings—all called together by the cries of the chickadees. Keeping a safe distance, they raised their voices in loud, abusive calls. The blue jays especially were filled with fury.

"If birds could swear, doubtless that owl listened to some very emphatic language," wrote Walton in recording the incident.

For twenty minutes the hemlock grove became an amphitheater of noisy bird calls—not the sweet sounds of the Ravenswood woodland chorus, but rather frenzied, grating shrills of anger.

The owl seemed bored, but was apparently fearless. Another ten minutes and all the birds disappeared, except two red-eyed vireos who continued to scold vigorously.

Walton soon understood why. About fifteen feet away their nest swung lightly from the limb of a beech and the owl had intruded on their territory. Observing closely, he suspected that the owl had become aware of the nest as he thrust out his head and swung it from side to side as if searching for something. After a short time, he found it and flew to the beech limb, landing a short distance from the nest. As he moved along in short hitches, the vireos changed their scolding to loud, piercing cries of alarm. Immediately all the birds returned, filling the air with screaming pandemonium. But they kept their distance. Undeterred by the clamor, the owl continued to approach the nest.

It was time for Walton to act. He rushed to the hemlock and shouted at the top of his voice, "Hold, there!"

The effect was instantaneous. The owl stopped short, crouched on the limb then twisted his impish face directly into the back of his neck and glared down at the intruder with a frightened look in his wide, expressive eyes. He tumbled forward off the limb, caught himself on his wings and floated noiselessly into the dark shadows of Magnolia Swamp. After he had gone and the birds quieted down, Walton examined the vireos' nest and found it empty. It was not yet completed, but the owl—the birds' arch enemy—had invaded their nesting grounds and they called upon their feathered friends to get rid of him.

"It is evident from what took place that birds of different species can communicate with each other," Walton wrote that day.

When all the birds had disappeared, Walton continued his search for a new sap orchard and found two red maples that had been tapped by woodpeckers, the belt of puncture nearly a foot in width. The yellow-bellied woodpecker that made the holes was nowhere around, leaving three hummingbirds and a red squirrel to fight for the sap buckets. Evidently the squirrel owned the territory and was more than willing to have woodpeckers tap the trees for his benefit, a benefit he did not intend to share with the hummingbirds. Driving them from one tree to another, the squirrel prevailed and claimed the spoils of victory. Walton watched as he raced around the tree, thrusting his tongue into the holes for the sweet sap, rather than eating from one spot as squirrels normally do.

According to ornithologists, woodpeckers tap trees so the sap will attract insects, their primary source of food. It is also their view that woodpeckers eat the soft bark, called the cambium layer, for food. Walton disagreed.

"While the woodpeckers do catch a fly now and then, it's evident even to a careless observer that it is the sap that is sought. I have seen them eat small pieces of the cambium layer, but I think they do so because the soft bark was soaked with sweet sap."

As he watched the squirrel enjoying the sap, Walton noticed a number of flies and hornets crawling on the bark of the maples and flying around the drill holes. Suddenly a hornet stung the squirrel on the ear. When he left to return to the cabin, the frantic squirrel was shaking his head wildly and, in his own way, telling the hornets what he thought of them.

A short distance from the hut, Walton found a pair of catbirds in trouble. Their nest was in a dense mass of shrubbery about eighty feet from the dooryard. The male catbird met him some distance from the nest and from his excited cries, Walton knew an enemy was threatening the security of their home. When he came in sight of the nest, he discovered the trouble. A black snake was making its way through the bushes toward the nest and the mother bird was waging a fierce but fruitless battle.

Their hero solved the problem with one quick blow. The nest contained four eggs and, for the time being at least, they were safe. In due time the baby catbirds arrived.

One moonlight night about ten o'clock there was a great outcry from their parents. Walton sprang from his hammock as one of the catbirds flew to the bushes within three feet of his head, frantically calling for his help. When he came in sight of the nest, he saw a snake dropping to the ground. One of the young birds was missing. A hurried search beneath the bushes in the dim light was unsuccessful. The snake had silently and swiftly disappeared with his victim.

Because the catbirds were long-time pets, Walton vowed to save the other three from a similar fate. He removed the nest from the tree to a covered box in the cabin. The parents followed him to the cabin door but did not protest. The next morning before sunrise, he was awakened by their cries. While he dressed they flew from cabin to hammock, hammock to cabin, calling him to hurry up and bring out their babies. Both had insects in their bills.

Rather than take the nest back to the tree, Walton placed it in a clump of bushes close to the cabin. When it was secured, the parents gave the three babies their breakfast. This routine was followed daily until the young birds were old enough to fly.

One Sunday about 200 visitors inspected the nest as the old birds looked on. They didn't protest or show fear as they knew "their hero" would protect their little ones.

Another example of bird intelligence became part of Walton's voluminous nature study.

A feisty red squirrel named Tiny reigned supreme over the dooryard.

Chapter 10
A Chip off the Old Block

Walton thought the red squirrel was the smartest animal on Cape Ann. From his notes, it is easy to see why he felt that way.

Having studied the three species of tree squirrels inhabiting Ravenswood—the red, gray and flying squirrel—he focused on the intelligence and energies of the red, smallest of the three.

"His life during the spring and summer months is a grand hurrah," he wrote, "but in the fall he sobers down and plods and toils in his harvest fields like a thrifty farmer."

Characterized by experts as "disreputable," the red squirrel was considered somewhat of a villain. Charges against him included theft from vegetable gardens and attacks on bird nests. At first Walton believed these stories but, after observing the behavior of those in Ravenswood, he changed his mind. He found, in fact, they did little harm to farmers' crops and were never harmful to birds, their eggs or their young. In his opinion this negative label was false, a view perpetuated by writers recycling the opinions of others rather than learning the facts for themselves through personal observation. In a column in *Forest and Stream*, he made his view quite clear.

"I know that my position in relation to the red squirrel's destruction of songbirds will be sharply criticized by those who believe in its total depravity. But the truth is that I describe wildlife just as I find it, not as some books say I ought to find it."

For years he had watched the reds chasing birds in the dooryard, thinking they would be injured, if not killed, when caught. Then he learned differently. Twice one summer he saw a red squirrel pounce on a young twohee bunting and both times let it go unharmed.

"It was evident that he did not intend to hurt the bird but merely desired to frighten it away," he wrote, confessing, "Now my eyes are open and I am heartily ashamed of myself."

Walton arrived at this conclusion by keeping a detailed record of the birds that nested near the cabin, stating that "probably every nest was known and visited by the red squirrel." During a fifteen-year study, the list grew to include three chestnut-sided warblers, one black-throated green warbler, two oven birds, four vireos, one Canada fly-catching warbler, two robins, two towhee buntings, one catbird, two Wilson's thrush and one indigo bird.

According to Walton's journal, the true enemies of Ravenswood's birdlife were the hawk, owl, crow, snake, stoat, cat, white-footed mouse—and the mischievous boy who absconded with his boot full of chickadees.

It always puzzled Walton that birds were not afraid of the red squirrel, expert opinion notwithstanding. When any of the afore-mentioned predators entered the dooryard while they were rearing their young, feathers flew in all directions. But the red squirrel came and went without protest, indicating that none of the birds considered him a foe. Whenever he found one around a bird's nest, it turned out to be simply a matter of curiosity on the squirrel's part. Frequently chickadees nested in a box in a nearby oak, and the red that ruled the dooryard peered into the nest several times a day. But he never harmed the birdlings and even with his noisy, rachet-like chatter, posed no threat to the doting parents.

Walton's journal described an incident involving a red and three young red-eyed vireos. One day as the birds squirmed about in the confinement of a pensile nest hanging from the fork of a small choke cherry tree, they were visited by one of these bushy-tailed rodents. Stretching his full length along a limb above the tiny trio, he looked down at them for two full minutes, Walton wrote, noting that the Peeping Tom made no attempt to disturb the defenseless birds.

His journal also told of a "tenement house" in a tall white pine occupied by oven birds and red squirrels. Three baby thrush-like birds nested on the ground floor while high above in the tree top, four small bundles of fur enjoyed their room with a view. Both species are noisy—usually heard before seen—which must have created bedlam when the young acted up. But like most apartment-dwellers on the human scale, the families were friendly and got along well together.

Perhaps his tenacity as a fighter is what earned the red squirrel a bad reputation. His claws are as sharp as needles and his muscular form becomes electrified at times. Watching his defense against his great gray cousin and other threatening wildlife, Walton thought him the bravest thing in the forest.

"When pursued by a dog he makes a dash for the nearest tree. He does not, like the gray squirrel, seek a hiding place in the top of the tree; he is far too bold for that. He stops on a low limb just out of reach and fairly boils over with rage and fury—barking, spitting and making furious rushes as if he intended to come right down the tree and whip that dog. He violently jerks his tail and pounds the limb with his hind feet, a picture of impudent, fiery energy."

Because he was no match for the red in tree-top speed trials, the gray usually kept to the ground where his long leaps gave him the advantage over his combative little foe. Watching many of these sprinting matches in his dooryard, Walton was able to study the competitors at great length and, as his entries reveal, their antics could be quite entertaining.

When the red surprised a gray helping himself to food on his turf one day, he considered it "stealing." Walton stood by watching the mad rush around the cabin, the gray struck dumb with terror, the red hot at his heels "yelling like a little demon." After several narrow escapes, the gray surrendered the food and raced off. The red took it to a limb and devoured it, all the while mumbling to himself about "that low-down gray thief."

Only once during his many years of observation did Walton see a gray squirrel instigate a fight with a red. The gray was a mature male three times the size of the red, a tough old warrior he named Bismarck, who at the time laid claim to the dooryard.

Evidently it was hunger and desperation that set off the battle on that cold, drizzly winter day. The fray was over bread. The red was energized to a frenzy, his movements almost too quick for the eye. At no time did the gray have a ghost of a chance to win. Observing from the cabin window, all Walton saw was a bounding mass of red and gray. When it was over, the snow was crimson with the blood of the defeated gray, who fled ahead of a gory, tell-tale trail. Bismarck didn't appear to be seriously hurt and remained out in the freezing weather licking his wounds rather than retreating to his nest.

In his findings, Walton opined that reds seldom chased the grays unless the latter entered their territory as was the case just cited. With a few exceptions wild animals laid claim to farms, gardens and wood lots, assuming exclusive property rights over these areas which became their nesting sites. It was highly unusual, he noted, to find two woodchuck holes near each other, or two rabbit burrows.

Bismarck owned a fruit farm, his trees yielding an autumn bounty of apples, nuts and cones. Other reds respected the rules of the animal kingdom and did not invade his territory unless there was a food shortage on theirs. Such was the situation one winter following a nut crop failure when an adventuresome young red scrambled up one of Bismarck's trees. A ferocious fight broke out, costing the old warrior the tip of his tail and his antagonist his life.

From his study of Bismarck, Walton concluded that many of the squirrel's actions were based on thought, logic and memory the same as humans. This judgment was formed after a few carefully-monitored surveillances.

Each time Walton threw him a nut or piece of bread, Bismarck went into "his thinking act." By that Walton meant the squirrel picked up the food and ran to a nearby boulder where he stopped briefly to consider a good hiding place. Deciding on a particular spot, he raced directly to it and hid the treat under leaves or pine needles, then returned to the dooryard for more. No two nuts or bits of bread were ever hidden in the same place.

Several times Walton tested the perseverance and energy of the busy little worker by counting the number of trips he made from market to cupboard. The greatest total was fifty-one. As he watched this bustling activity, he took note of the squirrel's hiding places as best he could. Later he saw Bismarck return to many sites, remembering most and no doubt led to others by his keen sense of smell.

Bismarck was a thrifty manager. As long as food was available in the dooryard, he did not disturb his hidden stores. He called on Walton early each morning and when he found him at breakfast under the trees, he scurried to a limb over his head. With an air of coquettishness, he gazed down longingly as if to ask, "breakfast for two?" If Walton didn't respond, he scampered off to retrieve a hidden nut, nosed it out and returned to the limb where he chewed away, scattering bits of shell onto the breakfast table below.

"He's very sociable when he eats," noted Walton. "He stops now and then to say something to me. I do not understand his exact language, but I know by his tone that he means to be friendly."

Bismarck didn't always store bread beneath pine needles or leaves; sometimes the trees about the cabin became his larder. To lodge it firmly in the fork of small limbs, he lifted the twigs with his hands and pushed the bread firmly in place with his nose. He also hid mushrooms in trees by dropping the stem between the prongs of a forked branch if there was enough cap to hold it in place. If not, he simply stored it under the twig as he did the bread. Blue jays did not bother the mushrooms, but they did go after his bread supply which caused many a fight between the two.

How Bismarck learned about edible mushrooms was a mystery to Walton. Not only did he know the good from the bad, but also exactly when to pick them. If left in the ground too long, they'd spoil; gathered shortly after they appeared, they'd remain good for a few days. And he knew how to economize when eating them. He didn't begin with the fresh ones, he knew they would keep. Instead, he selected those that would soon decay, much like a prudent housewife.

The fact that Walton never saw a tooth mark by a squirrel, mouse or mole on any of the poisonous varieties growing in Ravenswood reaffirmed his belief that birds and animals possess certain knowledge inherent in wildlife just as people experience in the human condition.

While on a hike with the Appalachian Mountain Club, Walton met a college professor who was an expert on the fleshie fungi. During a conversation, Walton told his companion that he ate only those mushrooms approved by squirrels and no others. The professor felt this to be a risky practice, stating that squirrels could eat poisonous ones that might kill humans.

"I have found the squirrels all right and I feel no fear when eating what they eat," Walton replied, rightly or wrongly.

When Bismarck first visited the hermitage, he was an old bachelor or a widower. For three years he lived the life of a loner, eating by himself in the dooryard, hoarding food for the winter, and sleeping alone in a nearby pine tree nest.

During the spring of the fourth year, he took a mate but it proved to be an unusual liaison—at least for awhile. When his bride attempted to join him in the dooryard, Bismarck snarled at her and chased her spiraling up and down tree trunks to escape his abuse. At times their speed was so swift they became a lightening-fast band of brown racing up and down the tree. After one such incident, Bismarck did not allow her into the dooryard for two weeks. When peace was finally restored, they ate alongside each other, Bismarck growling and scolding while his poor, abused wife remained meekly silent. In an effort to make him happy, she built a neat, little nest in a hemlock in the swamp where, in early April 1900, two sons were born.

Bismarck didn't pay much attention to his family that first summer, preferring his bachelor life instead. During the day he spent most of his time chasing birds, crows and other squirrels from the dooryard and at night retired to his own nest alone.

When the harvest season drew near, he accepted his responsibilities and behaved more like a family man. He helped his mate dig a storehouse in the trunk of an old hemlock on a hillside at the edge of the swamp. The work took three days. When the hazelnuts were ripe, they began to fill their larder, Bismarck gathering them about the cabin, his mate around her nest. The old-timer did a lot of running since he carried only one nut at a time and always worked under pressure, scurrying to and fro at top speed. Walton noticed that he left many nuts on the bushes. Upon investigation he found a worm in each one—a good reason for rejection, he thought. As the husks seemed perfect, he assumed it was Bismarck's keen sense of smell that culled out the wormy rejects.

After the hazelnuts were stored, the pair collected beechnuts in a similar manner, or at least they attempted to. Competition from belligerent blue jays limited their supply. By beating the squirrels' legs with their wings, the birds launched a bitter attack against the Bismarcks. But a healthy acorn crop soon came in and helped fill their storehouse, thanks to the abundance of nut-bearing oak trees on Cape Ann.

In gathering this ready crop, Bismarck again impressed Walton with his keen wit and hard work. Across the road from the cabin, four large northern red oaks yielded a bountiful harvest of the sweet, reddish-brown nut. Beneath the limbs on the south side was a carpet of pine needles, on the north a dense thicket of catbrier. The shrewd old squirrel didn't drop a single nut into the briers but carried one at a time to the clearing before tossing it to the ground. Could human intelligence do more? Walton wondered.

For the most part, the two baby squirrels remained in the nest during harvest time. From time to time they followed their mother to a nut tree, but were so noisy she feared they'd attract enemies so she scooted them home. When the storehouse was well stocked, the parents made a winter nest in the same tree and the entire family kept warm and well-fed during the cold, wintry weather. Bismarck's bachelor days were over.

One season there was famine on the land, providing Walton further insight into the resourcefulness of the red squirrel. In September the old warrior realized nuts were scarce and was forced to substitute pine cones, small bones and corn gathered from the dooryard. During the winter he supplemented his diet with frozen barberries, choke cherries and the berries of greenbrier and staghorn sumac. And he visited the dooryard for handouts.

For years Walton scattered pieces of bread and sweets across the yard for birds and animals. In addition he wired a large loaf of bread to a post near the cabin door. This groaning board was for the enjoyment of all comers; they could eat all they wanted "at table," but were not allowed carry the loaf away.

One blustery, rainy day Walton looked out the window and saw Bismarck sitting by the bread, not eating but "whimpering like a little child."

"He was telling me in squirrel language that it was cold, wet and almost night, and that I ought to give him some bread to take home to his family," wrote the tender-hearted hermit. "I understood his appeal and tossed him a biscuit and he scampered away chuckling over his good luck."

Thereafter all through the winter, in fair weather and foul, Bismarck begged Walton for bread to take home, always chattering gleefully when he got it.

"Perhaps he was laughing at me for being an easy mark, or it may have been squirrel talk for 'I thank you a thousand times.' However that may be, he was welcome for I thought of the baby squirrels at home half-starving on a cone-seed diet."

With the melting of snow, the resourceful little survivor ate pussy-willow buds, wintergreen and partridgeberries in addition to tapping maples and birches for sap. The latter caused Walton to wonder: did the red squirrel learn how to tap trees from the American Indian, or did the Indian learn from the squirrel?

The story of Bismarck through a year of famine is the story of other red squirrels on Cape Ann. For the attentive Gloucester naturalist, it was another eye-opener in his study of the mental acuteness of wildlife.

Walton was outraged at what he called a "foolish state law" that decimated the population of red squirrels and other wildlife during his years at Ravenswood. In 1889 the Massachusetts General Court declared a five-year moratorium on small game in Essex, Rockport and all of Gloucester, except Ward 8 where the little cabin was located. As a result of this legislation, sportsmen from closed areas descended upon Ravenswood and its environs, destroying nearly all the game and a great many songbirds.

When their forest playground became a killing field, the habits of squirrels changed. At the sound of a gun, they made a bee-line for their hiding places. They were forced to harvest their nut crops at night rather than during daylight hours. Sleeping in the open during harvest season, Walton listened for hours to the plop of falling nuts which the industrious, but wary, squirrels dropped from nearby oaks.

The story of Bismarck appeared in Walton's book while the old warrior was "still in the land of the living," having been his wild friend for more than ten years.

"He has cost me many dollars and has not paid a cent in the coin of the realm" he told readers good-naturedly. "However, I owe him for teaching me and I am ready to balance the books and exchange receipts."

After a decade of ownership, Bismarck surrendered the cabin dooryard to his offspring, Tiny, much like a father turns over his business to a son at retirement. When he assumed full possession, the heir to the throne proved to be a chip off the old block. His "no trespassing" edict was strictly enforced and applied to all—even his own family. Walton was often amused to see grizzly old Bismarck run for his life when Tiny caught him overstepping the lines of demarcation. In protecting his newly-acquired kingdom, the feisty little sovereign fiercely attacked any squirrel that did not heed his first warning.

Tiny faced one of his most difficult challenges when a monstrous wharf rat wandered into the dooryard one day. What brought him to the Ravenswood forest was a mystery. When he happened upon the hermit's cornucopia of bread, wheat, corn, meat and birdseed, he probably thought he'd discovered the mythical land of milk and honey. Since the dock-side prowler foraged under the cover of darkness, it was several days before he clashed with Tiny. Two nights of feasting obviously made the rat think he could support his family on the buffet he'd discovered in the woods, so he brought along his mate on his next visit. But Walton, keenly aware of the goings on in his dooryard, was on guard. He trapped the female, but her spouse was too crafty for him. Later the rat became bold enough to feed in the daytime which brought about his battle with Tiny.

One morning Walton and several tourists from a resort hotel looked on as the huge rodent fed from the loaf of bread. Suddenly, a war cry was heard from the trees as Tiny sprang to a limb about six feet above the bread and exploded into a rage, pounding and shouting profanities at the intruder below. The rat looked up, gave the angry squirrel an unworried glance, and returned to his meal. It never occurred to him to be afraid of such an insignificant little foe.

Tiny raced down the tree trunk, landing on the ground about four feet from the rat which stood on his hind feet and squealed a warning.

"Rats are great fighters," said Walton's lady visitor. "The poor little squirrel will be killed."

Walton grinned and offered to bet on the squirrel. But, before the woman could respond, the battle was on. A brown bundle whirled in a cloud of pine needles as Tiny fought like a cyclone. The rat soon learned that his little antagonist was not to be reckoned with and made desperate attempts to escape. Finally the struggle sent them both hurling against a stone wall, leaving a trail of blood in their wake. When the rat finally managed to break away and disappear into a small crevice, Tiny returned to the bread, none the worse from the fierce struggle. He had restored his supremacy over the dooryard and the rat never returned. He either died from the effects of Tiny's savage bites or, if he survived, sought his meals elsewhere.

Tiny was not always full of fight. Like his father, he did not harm birds. Walton watched with interest his budding friendship with a young twohee bunting who dropped in for a share of the groaning board one day. When Tiny approached, he expected the bird to fly away. Instead she set her wings and lowered her head in preparation for battle. Tiny sat up, placed his forepaws firmly on his chest, and looked down at the gamely little bird with wide-eyed wonder. But still she did not yield; she simply returned to the bread. Tiny brought his paws down hard on the ground in an attempt to frighten her away. Again the spunky little bunting set her wings and lowered her head, ignoring his threat.

Tiny sat up tall and looked the little trespasser over. This time Walton detected a bemused expression on the squirrel's face that said as plain as words that he admired her courage. Tiny then crept quietly to the opposite side of the bread loaf and allowed the bunting to eat unmolested. After this episode, the two ate together whenever they chanced to be in the dooryard at the same time.

The combative Tiny did not allow other birds near the bread, however, and Walton thought he would forget his feathered friend when the buntings returned in the following spring migration. He was wrong.

"Tiny knew the little bird at once and chuckled some kind of greeting," he noted, "and the bunting said something in bird language that seemed to my ears to express joy."

Walton's notes were full of stories about the resourcefulness and wit of red squirrels, not only Bismarck and Tiny, but many others who remained nameless. He eagerly pursued their antics and behavioral patterns, especially when they faced unusual situations. A case in point is worth mentioning.

In his attempt to feed the birds in Ravenswood, Walton maintained a ready supply of hempseed in the dooryard. The red squirrels and chipmunks also liked this treat and unless he stood guard, they'd take the lion's share. The chipmunks especially were hoarders; they stuffed their pouched cheeks and returned again and again for more. When Tiny was present, however, these animals didn't attempt to take the hempseed. He didn't harm the birds and seemed to know the seeds belonged to them, however, he was not above taking some himself.

In order to save the seeds for the birds, Walton constructed a make-shift bird-feeder by placing a wire netting over a shallow box. This allowed birds access to the grains, while at the same time, prevented animals from poking their noses through the mesh. The chipmunks at first appeared puzzled then, one after another, gave up and turned to the corn. When Tiny found the bird-feeder, he got mad. He thrust his nose against the wire netting and bit into it savagely. When Walton, watching nearby, laughed, the pugnacious little animal instantly stopped and glared at him. He seemed to realize the old man was responsible for his dilemma, and in three bounds he landed on the trunk of a pine tree. Running along a limb just over Walton's head, he pounded his feet and pumped his tail as if he were about to attack.

After about ten minutes of frenzy, he quieted down and returned to the box. He poked at the wire for a short time, then sat up with his paws planted across his chest and "fell into a brown study."

Then, to Walton's great surprise, he suddenly grasped the feeder and flipped it over. Pecking away at the seeds on the ground, he stopped from time to time to fling a few choice words in his tormentor's direction, all the while jerking his tail defiantly. For a week or more Walton allowed the impish Tiny to turn the container over because he wanted his visitors to see him in action. Later he secured it firmly to the ground. But Tiny did not give up. One day Walton returned to find the ground dug up underneath the box and a hole gnawed through the bottom.

He then tested the animal's intelligence by stretching a chord between two trees and suspending an open box halfway across. Tiny saw birds eating from the feeder and seemed to suspect another trick. He ran up one of the trees and found a slender limb that bent under his weight, allowing him drop easily into the box. After watching him use this highway several times, Walton cut the branch away. When Tiny found a fresh stub instead of a limb, he was not happy.

"He swore at me, if a squirrel can swear, for twenty minutes," Walton reported.

But Tiny was not done yet. His next move was to investigate the line supporting the box. In an attempt to reach the seed via this route, he started out from where the line was attached to the trees. When he had ventured across only a foot or so, the line turned, sending him sprawling to the ground. Three frustrating attempts ended in failure. Each time he picked himself up and tried again. The fourth time when the line turned, he clung to it and made his way to the receptacle hand-over-hand, his rump sashaying in the breeze. For his outstanding performance, Walton thought he deserved a reward and allowed him to eat from the feeder at his pleasure.

As November approached, Tiny made a cozy nest of moss, leaves and grass in the limb of a pine tree that spread over the dooryard. One morning when Walton returned, he found empty shells on the ground and fragments of the nest hanging from the tree.

"Some wretch had shot the nest to pieces when I was absent," he lamented.

Tiny made another nest in a nearby pine, where he was still in residence when the hermit's book containing a story about him was released in March 1903. At that time Tiny was a childless widower. His family, including Bismarck, had been shot to death by the hunters who swarmed through the magnolia woods when they became the only hunting grounds on Cape Ann.

As noted by his friend Frank Bolles, Walton was considered one of the fauns of the forest. Nowhere is this more evident than in his own poignant words about the common thread that bound him to the little red squirrel.

"Tiny is now an orphan, a widower and is also childless," he confided to his journal. "He occupies in squirrel life the same relative position that the hermit occupies in human life. Tiny's misfortune has brought the man and squirrel a little nearer together."

Walton named the fox Triplefoot because she traveled on three feet.

Chapter 11
Triplefoot

On a bitter cold January morning, the hermit peered through the frozen glass of his cabin window. Two inches of fresh snow covered the silent landscape. Viewing the peaceful winter scene, he noticed a cluster of lacy medallions, made by the footprints of a fox, around the base of a tree where he had nailed a chunk of left-over meat.

Under his watchful eye, an unusual pattern of tracks in the snow—three prints followed by a space, another three prints followed by a space—raced from the tree down the old highway. Having been a hunter in Maine, he had no difficulty understanding their significance. The fox had been trapped sometime in the past and had sacrificed a foot in order to live another day.

The fox, a female, was no stranger to Walton. Months before he had made her acquaintance in the dooryard. He named her Triplefoot because she traveled on three feet. She was living a charmed life he thought at the time, as hunters had been unable to shoot her so far, although for more than a year she remained the only fox in Ravenswood and the hounds pursued her night and day.

On the morning Walton found Triplefoot's tracks trotting down Old Salem Road, he decided to trail her to her den. It was a good tracking snow, leading him down the hill to Solomon's Orchard where wild apple trees and two cellar ruins were all that remained of a long-ago farm. The fox did some foraging under the barberry bushes, he noticed. Several drops of blood and feather-light prints of tiny feet and tail told the story of a wood mouse's last stand.

As he searched for the trail out of the orchard, Walton heard the barking of excited hounds. From their sound, he knew they had picked up Triplefoot's scent and were hot on her trail. Within seconds they bounded into sight and raced past him toward Magnolia Swamp. Walton pushed his way through the dense shrubbery, following the well-defined tracks—now of two dogs and a fleeing three-footed fox.

By the direction of her flight, Walton realized Triplefoot was heading for water to lose her scent. The tracks led him through the swamp and over the ridge to Wallace's Pond. But the cold weather was against the fleeing quarry. All the brooks and ponds were frozen solid. After crossing Magnolia Avenue and finding a hidden lily pond also iced over, she ran full tilt along the ridges of Mount Ann. Her destination was Coffin's Beach two miles distant by the way the crow flies. For Walton it was a long, weary tramp but he persevered, determined to stay with her to the finish.

By the time he reached the sand dunes behind the beach, the morning sun had melted the snow. Here the trail ended. Triplefoot had thrown the hounds off, and Walton right along with them. Not a sign of her three-legged gait could be seen in the sparkling white sand. Her successful escape once again characterized the craftiness of the entire fox family—the reds and grays of New England, as well as those roaming the Arctic of the Far North Tundra.

Walton had to make a decision, give up and go home or skirt the woods for Triplefoot's trail where she left the beach. Luck was with him when he chose the latter. In less than ten minutes, he came upon her tell-tale tracks leading back to Mount Ann and across Dyke's Meadow. They brought him again to Magnolia Swamp south of Solomon's Orchard then along the ridges near the old quarry. Dust was settling over Ravenswood when he found her den under a big boulder—only an eight-minute walk from his cabin. It had been a long, exhausting day for the resolute Mr. Walton who ended up somewhat miffed at having spent the whole day looking for something that was right in his own backyard.

Triplefoot reared three pups during the next season. As was the practice of new fathers, her mate provided food for the first few days, but then left most of this task to her. Being a foxy lady, she had put away two hens and a grouse—in cold storage, so to speak—so she could be with her young longer before she was forced to feed them alone. The pups stayed in the den for a month then ventured to the opening to play and feed. Walton spent many hours watching them through his long-distance lens.

One evening as he was standing on the high, flat top of the boulder over the den, one of the cubs came out and started up the ledge. When he saw Walton he stopped with his forepaws on the edge and looked him over. After the inspection he went back into the den and returned immediately with one of his siblings.

"The little imp had probably told his brother to come and see the comical two-legged beast," he noted in his journal. "The two cubs placed their feet on the ledge and looked at me for two solid minutes. They were not over six feet from me and looked as fat and stocky as two young pigs."

Like all female creatures in the wild, Triplefoot's life was one of anxiety and maternal care. Danger was her constant companion. When she hunted for wood mice, the hounds were sure to pick up her trail and she had to seek water to get away. If she turned to some farm yard, chances were she found herself looking into the muzzle of a shot gun.

Walton followed her activities closely.

"She was desperately wild and so were the little cubs when they were with her," he recorded, noting that her warnings of danger "worked like magic."

"The little ones would crouch and creep to the mouth of the den and disappear as silently as three ghosts."

One Sunday morning through his glass Walton saw the vixen return to the den empty-handed. The cubs came out and whined pitifully when they realized there would be no breakfast. She ordered them inside and then ran down the path to Fresh Water Cove. Walton knew that a large flock of barnyard fowl often strayed to the bushes near the highway and he knew that Triplefoot knew it, too. In twenty minutes she was back with a large white hen slung across her neck and called her young to breakfast under a hemlock.

One thing about Triplefoot's hunting practice puzzled the hermit. He couldn't understand why she did not go after poultry every day. Flocks from nearby farms could be found in every direction from the den. In his opinion it would have been an easy matter to snatch one from the bushes at any time. But again the lady proved foxy.

"She may have reasoned that a fowl now and then would not be missed while wholesale slaughter would attract attention and send the farmer hunting for her den.''

That fall only six months after their birth the cubs were killed and Triplefoot was left childless. Her mate was probably shot by hunters, too, Walton guessed, as he no longer saw him during his woodland walks.

But he continued to see Triplefoot. She seemed to understand that he alone did not covet her glossy pelt and set him apart from mankind in general. At times she appeared at the entrance of the den, standing quietly in the focus of his binoculars. Walton sensed that she knew he was watching but was not afraid. As happened on occasion with other animals, she often led pursuing hounds through the dooryard, knowing that if the caretaker was about he'd help throw them off her trail.

One fall Walton witnessed another of her many escapes. He was resting in the woods when he heard the yelps of dogs in Magnolia Swamp. Triplefoot was trying to throw them off but they stayed with her scent as she raced through the wetland. Near where Walton sat, a pine tree had been blown over by a storm. The trunk was suspended about two feet above the ground near the up-ended roots. Its top branches and foliage had fallen about ten feet over the edge of a deep ravine.

Listening to the clamor of the barking hounds, he spied Triplefoot racing through the distant woods. At break-neck speed, she passed close to the fallen pine and continued up a hill. Beyond was a valley and a small pond. Walton kept her in sight, assuming she was heading for the water to throw the dogs off. But this time he was wrong. At the top of the hill she stopped and looked around. She must have realized the man sitting on the rock was her friend from the cabin. She raced to the tree, ran along its sloping trunk and crawled up into the thick green branches above the chasm. There she waited.

In the heat of the chase, the hounds bolted past the tree, up over the hill and down the other side. Having lost both sight and smell, they climbed back up the hill and retreated, passing the tree along the way. But one suspected the tree might be harboring the fox and decided to investigate. Placing his paws on the trunk, he smelled along as far as he could reach, then gave up and trotted down the path to Western Avenue. Shortly Triplefoot emerged from the piney dell, having once again eluded her arch enemy.

In his closing remarks about Triplefoot, her kindred spirit mourned, "I wish I might end the story of this little three-footed fox in some happy way but truth has ordered it otherwise. She was shot when running before the hounds but was not immediately killed.

"I found her dead body while skirting Magnolia Swamp. She had crawled under a boulder and had slowly died from her wounds and exhaustion. I buried her and was glad that her beautiful robe and her mutilated body would not be separated in death."

Chapter 12
The Nature Fakers Controversy

Like others writing about nature at the turn of the century, Mason Walton became embroiled in what was known as "the nature fakers controversy." At issue was the psychological make-up of birds and animals. Was it intelligence or merely instinct that governed the behavior of the many species of wildlife roaming the hills, plains and vast wilderness of America? Was it acquired skill or irrational impulse that characterized the mating rituals, nesting habits, filial relationships, food sources, communication and migratory patterns of these awesome creatures?

Answers to these and similar questions soon became the focus of a heated literary debate between nature writers of every bent. For five long years, the subject was argued in many of the country's leading newspapers and magazines.

The highly-acclaimed naturalist, John Burroughs, started the controversy by writing an article entitled "Real and Sham Natural History" in the March 1903 issue of *Atlantic Monthly.*

"Animal behavior is simply the result of the adaptiveness and plasticity of instinct," he wrote, "not intelligence."

He then lodged a vigorous protest against what he considered "the growing tendency to humanize the lower animals."

In his opinion, "The animal has impulses and impressions where humans have ideas and concepts."

While not mentioning Walton by name or pseudonym, Burroughs bitterly attacked "the new school of nature writers or natural history romancers that reads into birds and animals almost the entire human psychology." But the reference clearly included *The Hermit* whose simple essays did not always agree with Burroughs' scientific views of wildlife.

As the dispute escalated, President Theodore Roosevelt joined in to support Burroughs. The two had helped create the wave of interest in nature and wildlife that was spreading across the American landscape in the mid-to-late 19th century. They considered themselves men with a scientific knowledge of nature whose observations were objective and writings, accurate. They felt writers like William Long, Ernest Seton, Charles Roberts, Jack London and Walton lacked such qualifications and were wrong in their perception of animal behavior.

When books by these authors began appearing in school classrooms and libraries across the country, Burroughs felt both students and the public were being deceived. To learn about the beauties of nature was one thing, he rebuked; to be presented fanciful stories as fact was something else. He charged that money alone was the reason behind the influx of nature stories and assailed their publishers as well as the writers. Burroughs' remarks raised a furor, setting off what the *New York Times* described as "The War of the Naturalists."

The severest criticism of all by Burroughs was aimed at Long, a Congregational minister from Stamford, Connecticut, who enjoyed a second career as a popular nature writer. In essence Burroughs said Long was an imitator and a liar, that his books were ridiculous and his sole purpose in writing them was for money. He accused Long of taking many of his ideas from Seton whom he also labeled a fraud.

Attacking a story Long wrote about older crows teaching their young to serve as look-outs, the famed naturalist scoffed, "The idea was a false one before Mr. Long appropriated it [from Seton] and it has been pushed to such length that it becomes ridiculous. There is not a shadow of truth in it. It is simply one of Mr. Seton's strokes of fancy."

Yet Burroughs acknowledged, "It is true that crows and jays might be called the spies and informers of the woods and that other creatures seem to understand the meaning of their cries, but who shall presume to say that they have been instructed in this vocation? What Mr. Long and Mr. Seton read as parental obedience is simply obedience to instinct."

He went on to say, "Mr. Long's book reads like that of a man who has really never been to the woods, but who sits in his study and cooks up these yarns from things he has read in *Forest and Stream* or in other sporting journals." This undoubtedly was a jab at Walton who responded in *The Hermit's* column.

"I do not care to express an opinion on either side at present, but do desire to call attention to some of Mr. Burroughs' false natural history." He then supported an assertion made by Long that robins were taught to sing by their parents.

When President Roosevelt read Walton's attack on Burroughs, he wrote a six-page letter to his friend, George Grinnell, publisher of *Forest and Stream*. Like other publishers, Grinnell received private letters from an angry President every time he disagreed with articles appearing in their publications. Roosevelt was upset by Walton's comments but, since he could not speak out publicly, he cautioned Grinnell to treat his letter privately. In it he ridiculed Walton's belief that birds teach their young to sing.

The *New York Times* ran a letter from naturalist John R. Spears, supporting the Hermit's views and applauding him for challenging Burroughs' knowledge of natural history.

When *A Hermit's Wild Friends*, published under Walton's real name, was released during the controversy, the Gloucester woodsman gained further credibility. A book reviewer for *Dial* magazine wrote that his stories "have the stamp of truth which only long and sympathetic intimacy can give. Consequently, they are the best sort both to enjoy and to make deductions from."

The debate pitting Burroughs and Roosevelt against some of the country's best known and loved nature writers was joined by editors, publishers and nature lovers, both pro and con. Some found the controversy amusing—intelligent men, many prominent figures in American life, arguing over the goings-on of porcupines and songbirds. Others attempted to reconcile Burroughs and Long because of their respect for the former and their affection for the books written by the latter.

In the final analysis, none of the nature writers was a deliberate fraud as charged by Burroughs: it was simply a matter of one's attitude toward nature—science versus sentiment.

Chapter 13
"The Hermit is Gone From Us"

As spring came to Ravenswood in 1917, the devastation of war-torn European cities and villages was a sharp contrast to the peaceful haven of Walton's woodland retreat. His home was now a log cabin more than twice the size of his first hut. The door opened into a "sunken living room," a large main room of concrete flooring. During the day sunlight brightened the inside through two small windows, one left of the door, the other in the middle of the right side wall. At night the warm glow of a kerosene lantern made cozy the rustic interior.

To hold the many books he'd accumulated over the years, shelves were built into a section of the left side wall. Next to these, toward the back of the cabin, was a kitchen range given to him by Mr. Hammond. Opposite, in the right corner of the room, was a cot and small chest of drawers, partitioned off to lend privacy to a small sleeping area. In the larger, open space furnishings were sparse: a bamboo settee for guests, a Morris chair for the host and, for writing and eating, a wooden table and chair. Along the right wall a box held an assortment of tools.

Outside, trellises were ready to support beans, wild grapes, and morning glories which surrounded the cabin each year. A capped smoke-stack of galvanized steel shot three feet into the air above the peak of the cedar shingled roof, the front of which extended two feet above the entrance to protect against bad weather. Over the door hung an inverted horseshoe, defying its superstitious symbolism of bad luck. Walton had no truck for such foolishness. He simply liked horseshoes; they reminded him of his farm in Maine.

Across the road under the oaks, wooden benches and a guest book greeted visitors. During his 33-year residency, the signatures revealed he welcomed an average of 4,000 people a year to his forest home, about 200 on Sundays.

When warm weather approached, this spring would be different at the Ravenswood hermitage. Walton's health was declining. A cold sent him to his cot to nap these days which he had never done in all his years of hermit life. He'd not had the time, nor the inclination; there were birds to watch, animals to track, records to keep, books to read and stories to write.

It had been more than thirty years since those miserable days when dyspepsia and catarrh drained his body strength and almost took his life. Although the illnesses never recurred to the extent they had in Boston, from time to time he'd been troubled with hay fever, but he usually shrugged it off, never allowing the discomfort to interfere with his daily activities.

As he lay on his cot in his small bed chamber in April of his seventy-ninth year, Walton was reminded of those long-ago days of infirmity when he could do nothing more than rest and let nature take its course. He did so now. But instead of improving, his condition worsened each day. What he first thought was a mild cold soon developed into a hacking cough, bringing up bloody phlegm and at times causing pain in his chest. Sometimes he felt flushed and feverish, at others he became chilled to the bone and could not seem to warm himself.

It was early in the evening of May 17 when his friend Arthur Homans found him, cold, hungry and very ill. Homans and his wife Lottie, his closest neighbors, lived on the corner of Old Salem Road and Western Avenue. They greeted him each morning as he limped past their house on the way to the city. Through the years he'd enjoyed many tasty meals at their kitchen table.

Concerned because she had not seen him for several weeks, Lottie sent her husband up to the cabin to check on the old man. Taking two neighbors with him, Homans, himself in his seventies, climbed the hill to the cabin. As the men approached the dooryard, the condition of the property indicated something was wrong.

An April nor'easter had blown away part of the wooden fence, scattering it, along with Walton's writing table and several bird houses into the nearby woods. The garden was not plowed which they thought unusual since he was among the first to make ready his spring planting. Homans feared the worse.

Pushing the door slightly ajar, he called to his friend. There was no answer. He stepped into the main room and called again. Again, there was no response. In the dusk it was difficult to see the details of the interior. Making his way to the back, Homans looked behind the wall. In the dim light his eyes fell upon the motionless form on the cot. He called one of the men to light the lamp on the table and bring it to him. Drawing close to the bed, he gazed anxiously into Walton's ashen face. Slowly, the eyes opened and the head turned toward the light. Confused and disoriented, the dying man did not know his visitors, nor even who or where he was.

Leaving him in the care of his neighbors, Homans hurried down the hill, ordered Lottie to take some hot soup up to the cabin, then rushed across the Cut to the City Hospital. An ambulance was dispatched immediately to Ravenswood.

Lottie and Arthur looked on sadly as Walton, frail and emaciated, was placed on a stretcher and lifted gently into the horse-drawn conveyance. Then the small group walked silently behind the wagon as it carried its burden down Old Salem Road. At the bottom of the hill, it turned left onto Western Avenue. When it reached their house, the Homans withdrew and watched as the driver guided the team of horses toward the hospital.

Located a mile west of the outer harbor, the City Home and Hospital were part of a complex serving the needs of Gloucester's poor. Officially called the Alms House, but more commonly the Poor Farm, it sprawled across twenty-three acres of farmland behind a massive rocky headland on the Annisquam River—two miles by the way the crow flies from the Ravenswood cabin. The homeless were sheltered in a large, white farmhouse, the sick tended in the attached three-story, block-shaped infirmary of red brick.

At the hospital the attending physician listened to Walton's chest and detected distortions in his breathing. Further examination led to a diagnosis of pneumonia, bronchitis, lung fever and congestion, the seriousness of which was compounded in people weakened by age and heart and lung ailments. Of the three, Walton fell victim to two; his bouts with catarrh and hay fever had impaired his lungs and now laid him low at age seventy-nine.

The physician treated his patient with large, hot flaxseed poultices and pectoral plasters to draw out the inflammation and lessen the discomfort in his chest. He was also given doses of cough syrup and other patent medicines free of opium, morphine and narcotic. But nothing helped. Walton died quietly in his sleep four days later, on May 21, 1917.

"The Hermit is Gone from Us" read a Boston headline the following day. In reporting the death, the journalist said he had many fond memories of an interview he'd had with Walton two years earlier and praised his love of nature and wildlife.

At the funeral, Gloucester's friendly hermit was eulogized by Mayor John Stoddard.

"Mason A. Walton, known for thirty years to the people of Gloucester as one of its respected citizens, has now been taken from our midst and leaves pleasant memories of a man who, although living the life of a hermit, was exceptionally interested in the welfare of this splendid city," said the Mayor.

"He was a great lover of children as well as nature and had the greatest respect for the little ones and their tender years, and an equal respect for the adults who were privileged to come in contact with him.

"It was my privilege to become acquainted with Mr. Walton on his arrival in Gloucester and, although being quite young, I recall my first visit, together with other children of my age, to the Hermit's cabin on Bond Hill and the very pleasant memories which I have held for the past twenty years, I shall always cherish.

"The passing away of this distinguished citizen takes from our midst one whose figure it was pleasing to greet on the Main Street as he was wont to make his visit each and every day on his little errands. He attracted the attention not only of the citizens of our city, but also of many people from other parts of the country who learned of him through the different newspaper articles which he had written and which are of great interest to nature lovers.

"As a representative of the people, I feel it my duty to add to this occasion by my presence and by paying my last respects for and in behalf of the City of Gloucester to this man who has been among us so many years and who was a respected and honored citizen."

Other tributes followed. Most spoke of their personal acquaintance with the man they called "the Hermit," listing the qualities that had endeared him to the citizens of Gloucester—his love for children, his interest in birds and wild animals, his intelligence and general store of knowledge and his "never-varying cheerfulness."

A suggestion was made that the hermitage be preserved as a tribute to Walton's memory, or that a tablet be placed on the big boulder nearby.

At the close of the service, a small band of mourners followed the funeral coach to the railroad station. Dr. Alfred Walton, a retired surgeon in Bangor, had arranged for his brother's burial in the family plot in Alton, Maine. There, beside his beloved wife Olive and the infant child he had never known, the body of Mason Augustus Walton was gently laid to rest on May 24, 1917.